Stop Attending Prospects and Sell to Your Customers

E. G. Filippini

Original Title: *Stop attending prospects and sell to your customers.*
Cover design: E. G. Filippini

1st printing: October 2024

© 2024 E. G. Filippini

ISBN 9798304167741

Independently published

All rights reserved. Under penalty of law, reproduction of this work in whole or in part by any means or process, including reprography and computer processing, or distribution of copies by public rental or lending, is strictly prohibited without written permission from the copyright holders.

STOP ATTENDING PROSPECTS AND
SELL TO YOUR CUSTUMERS

To my wife whom I love, respect and admire, for her dedication to me, as well as the tireless care in the health and education of our 3 children, throughout 18 years of marriage, who has remained steadfast by my side, supporting me and weathering the gales of every step we have taken in the good and not so good decisions that give us the best lesson of life.

Making me a better salesman and negotiator of life itself.

Index

Prologue 13

Gratefulness 16

Chapter 1: The importance of communication

1.1 Definition of communication in sales 18
1.2 The communication process: Elements and barriers 18
1.3 Importance of active listening 19
1.4 Verbal and nonverbal communication: Impact on sales 19
1.5 Communication and trust-building 19
1.6 Multichannel communication: Adapting to customer 20

Chapter 2: Personal image and its impact on sales

2.1 The importance of personal image in sales 22
2.2 Personal image components for sale 23
2.3 Adaptation of personal image 24
2.4 Strategies to improve and maintain a personal image of positive sales ... 25
2.5 Personal image case studies 27

Chapter 3: Body language and the importance of greeting

3.1 The importance of greeting in the sales process 30
3.2 Handshake positions and their meaning 31
3.3 Other aspects of body language in greeting 32
3.4 Adapting greeting and body language to different cultural contexts ... 33
3.5 Practical examples of greetings in different sales contexts 34

Chapter 4: The influence of personality on sales

4.1 What is personality and why is it important in sales? 37
4.2 Personality models and customer types 37
4.3 How to identify the customer's personality 39
4.4 Tailor your sales approach according to personality type 40
4.5 The seller's personality and its impact 41

Chapter 5: Psychology of human behavior

5.1 The psychology of purchasing decisions ... 44
5.2 Consumer behavior: Key psychological theories ... 45
5.3 The influence of cognitive biases on sales ... 46
5.4 Emotional selling ... 47
5.5 Sales psychology case studies ... 48

Chapter 6: Definition and types of customers

6.1 What is a customer: Definition and essential elements ... 50
6.2 Classification of customers according to their purchasing behavior ... 50
6.3 Customer segmentation by customer lifecycle ... 52
6.4 Classification of customers according to their value to the company ... 54
6.5 Psychological characteristics of clients ... 55
6.6 Case studies: Strategies adapted to types of clients ... 56

Chapter 7: Breaking the ice to strike up a conversation

7.1 The psychology of the first encounter ... 58
7.2 Icebreaker techniques ... 58
7.3 Overcoming initial barriers of resistance ... 60
7.4 Digital communication ... 61

Chapter 8: Active listening

8.1 What is active listening? ... 63
8.2 Benefits of active listening in sales ... 63
8.3 Active listening techniques ... 64
8.4 Obstacles to active listening and how to overcome them ... 65

Chapter 9: Consultative selling and the power of Storytelling

9.1 What is consultative selling? ... 68
9.2 Introduction to storytelling in sales ... 69
9.3 Storytelling strategies for consultative selling ... 70
9.4 Practical cases of Storytelling in consultative selling ... 71
9.5 Advanced storytelling techniques in consultative selling ... 72
9.6 Fundamental concepts of consultative selling ... 73
9.7 Step-by-Step consultative selling process ... 75
9.8 Practical examples of consultative selling in various sectors ... 76
9.9 Advanced techniques for maximizing the impact of consultative selling ... 78

Chapter 10: The Deming Chain and its application in sales

10.1 The Deming Chain: Concept and Fundamentals ... 80
10.2 Application of the PDCA cycle in the sales process ... 80
10.3 Practical implementation of the Deming chain in sales ... 82
10.4 PDCA cycle application examples ... 83
10.5 Long-Term benefits of the Deming chain ... 84

Chapter 11: Pipeline and Marketing

11.1 What is a sales pipeline? ... 86
11.2 Marketing strategies for each stage of pipeline ... 87
11.3 Key metrics for monitoring the sales pipeline ... 89
11.4 Technologies and tools for pipeline management and marketing ... 90
11.5 Advanced pipeline and integrated marketing strategies ... 91

Chapter 12: Cold calling

12.1 What is a cold call? ... 93
12.2 Preparing for successful cold calls ... 93
12.3 Strategies and techniques for successful cold calling ... 94
12.4 Cold calling script example ... 95
12.5 Example of using text messages via WhatsApp ... 97
12.6 Case study: Step-by-Step message creation to close a sale on WhatsApp ... 99

Chapter 13: Identifying and counterarguing objections

13.1 Understanding sales objections ... 103
13.2 Techniques for identifying objections ... 103
13.3 Techniques for counterarguing sales objections ... 106
13.4 Practical examples of counter-argumentation of objections in sales ... 109
13.5 Advanced strategies for converting objections in sales opportunities ... 110
13.6 Case study: Script for handling sales objections ... 111

Chapter 14: Closing sales

14.1 The importance of closing in the sales process ... 114
14.2 Sales closing strategies: Main techniques ... 114
14.3 Psychology of the sales closing: Understanding the customer behavior ... 118
14.4 Practical examples of Step-by-Step sales closing ... 119

Chapter 15: The importance of after-sales

15.1 Customer loyalty: Beyond the initial sale … 121
15.2 Improving customer experience: Ensuring satisfaction and trust … 121
15.3 Opportunities for upselling and cross-selling … 122
15.4 Encourage positive recommendations and testimonials … 122
15.5 Collecting feedback for continuous improvement … 122
15.6 Building a long-term relationship and competitive differentiation … 123
15.7 Strategies for effective after-sales … 123
15.8 Case study: After-sales follow-up for loyalty and sale of recommended … 124

Chapter 16: The importance of customer service and attention in after-sales

16.1 Customer service as a pillar of after-sales … 130
16.2 Key components of good customer service in aftersales … 130
16.3 Strategies for providing exceptional after-sales service … 131
16.4 The importance of customer satisfaction in the after-sales service … 132
16.5 How to turn aftersales into a competitive advantage … 133
16.6 Aftermarket customer service case studies … 133
16.7 Measurement and continuous improvement of after-sales service … 134

Chapter 17: Customer retention and reactivation strategies

17.1 The importance of customer retention … 137
17.2 Customer retention strategies … 137
17.3 Reactivation of inactive clients … 139
17.4 Measuring the success of retention and reactivation strategies … 140
17.5 Customer retention and reactivation use cases … 140

Chapter 18 - Practical sales exercises for real situations … 142

Chapter 19 - Case studies … 168

Final summary … 182

Epilogue … 186

Glossary … 189

Prologue

"stop Attending prospects and Sell to your customers"

From the moment I decided to enter the world of sales, I was confronted with a reality that many salespeople know all too well: the constant struggle to attract and convert prospects into customers. It is a cycle that seems to have no end and that, for many, becomes frustrating, exhausting and even demotivating. You invest time, effort, and resources in presenting products or services to people who seem interested, but who in the end don't make the purchase decision. At worst, you realize that many of those prospects were never really interested. It's a common phenomenon, especially for those just starting their career in sales or for those who have followed a traditional, ineffective path.

The truth is that all salespeople have witnessed how our list of prospects grows, but our closing figures do not do so at the same pace. This is where an important reflection arises: are we focusing our efforts on the right people? And more importantly, are we selling or simply serving prospects who won't become customers?

This book is born from that reflection, but also from an urgent need that I detected both in my personal career and in that of many other salespeople with whom I have had the opportunity to work. The need to learn to accurately identify who is a potential prospect and who is a real customer. The need to sharpen our tools and techniques so that our effort is not diluted in hundreds of conversations that come to nothing but is concentrated on those business relationships that can really generate value, both for us and for our customers.

Throughout my years in sales, I've come across a lot of misconceptions about what it really means to sell. In many cases, selling is associated only with the ability to persuade, with the ability to convince someone that they need something they weren't really looking for. And although persuasion is undoubtedly an important tool in this field, it is not the only one, far from the most relevant. Effective selling isn't about trying to convert every person you meet into a customer, it's about making authentic connections with those who truly value what you offer.

One of the most common mistakes we make as salespeople, especially at the beginning of our careers, is to think that the number of prospects is the most important thing. We believe that the more people who hear about our offer, the greater our chances of closing a sale. And while there might be some truth to this, the reality is that not all prospects are created equal, and many of them will never become customers, no matter how much time and effort we put into them.

That's why the focus of this book is different. It's not about teaching you how to attract more prospects, but about learning how to identify and focus on those who really have the potential to become loyal and satisfied customers. Because, at the end of the day, it's not about how many doors you knock on, it's about how many open and let you in.

For a long time, the sales industry has been obsessed with the notion that more is always better. More prospects, more calls, more meetings, more emails. But what if I told you that selling more doesn't depend on serving more prospects, but on being more selective with those you decide to sell to? What if you focused your efforts on building meaningful relationships with those customers who really need what you offer, rather than trying to sell to everyone?

This approach is not only more efficient, but also more satisfying. When you start selling to the right customers, the sales process is no longer a never-ending, stressful race, and becomes a smooth, natural, and most importantly, profitable experience. Instead of being trapped in a cycle of constant persuasion, you find yourself collaborating with people who value what you offer, who appreciate your expertise, and who are willing to invest in what you provide.

This is where many salespeople get lost: they believe that selling is synonymous with "cating" to an endless number of prospects who show interest but are not really engaged. My purpose with this book is to help you change that mindset. I want you to see selling not as a process of serving endless prospects, but as an art in which you learn to spot and work with real customers.

One of the most important aspects I've discovered in my career is that the prospects who seem most interested aren't always the ones who buy. This truth was hard to accept at first, but when I realized that superficial interest doesn't necessarily translate into sales, everything changed. From that moment on, I decided to focus my efforts on those customers who demonstrated a deeper commitment, those who were not only interested in the product, but understood its value and how it could impact their lives or businesses.

One concept that we will address throughout this book is the value of the "ideal customer". Many times, in the desire to increase our sales, we try to sell to everyone. However, not all prospects are good customers. In fact, some of them can become a source of frustration and waste of time if they are not suitable for the product or service you offer. Part of what you'll learn here is how to define your ideal customer and how to focus exclusively on attracting and selling them.

As you apply these principles, you'll find that sales become simpler and more natural. It's not about forcing anyone to buy something they don't need or want, but about offering solutions to people who are really looking for what you offer. This is one of the main differences between the traditional sales approach and the approach I present to you in this book: here you will learn how to sell strategically, how to focus on the right people, and how to close more sales with less effort.

On the following pages, we'll explore in detail the strategies that will help you stop wasting time with prospects and sell effectively to your customers. From how to identify your ideal customer, to negotiation techniques that will allow you to close more sales successfully, this book will provide you with all the tools you need to transform your sales approach.

We'll also talk about the importance of building long-term relationships with your customers. Many times, salespeople focus so much on closing a sale that they forget the importance of nurturing the relationship with the customer after the transaction. A satisfied customer not only buys again, but also recommends you to others. That is why one of the pillars of this book is to teach you how to build trust and loyalty in your customers, so that they become ambassadors of your brand and help you grow in a sustained way.

Finally, I want to remind you that this book is not just for beginners. If you already have sales experience but feel like you're stuck in a rut or that your efforts aren't paying off as well as you'd hope, this approach can also be a refreshing change for you. Sometimes, all we need to do to improve our bottom line is to adjust our approach and change the way we approach sales.

With my experience that I share with you here, it will help you to finish this book, not only will you be more successful in your sales, but you will also enjoy the process more. Selling doesn't have to be an arduous and exhausting task. In fact, when you focus on the right customers and use the right strategies, it can be a rewarding experience, both for you and your customers.

So, I invite you to leave behind the mentality of "serving prospects" and to get into a more effective and satisfying approach: that of selling to your customers.

Welcome to a new chapter in your sales career!

Gratefulness

In the world of sales, you develop according to the environment in which you find yourself and each of the people around you.

Each person with whom one gets involved represents a part of education and training in life, in which they become a guide, teacher, coach or mentor. The great influences (my good Friends) that contribute to personal development, are the ones from whom one strengthens their pillars of personality and forges their course.

Therefore, of first and greatest gratitude it is to my own family, my Parents, Brothers and Brothers-in-Law to whom I have a great stimulus, that thanks to each of them I obtained strong foundations of great value based on constructive and self-critical analysis, solid human values, good behavior in society and above all excellent self-esteem, which has become my core part to know how to face any situation that has arisen.

I have had the joy of meeting over time excellent Teachers within my professional education from whom I received countless tips to excel and improve in everything I have come to do.

Later in the work environment, each of my Bosses, Supervisors, Coaches, Managers, Directors and some CEOs with whom I have come to collaborate and extended their hand to me with a firm and trustworthy greeting to climb to better positions within the companies in which I worked, as well as their teachings that many occasions with their own example of doing things, the way they behaved in a group and the subtlety with which they got involved with all their employees; I learned, understood, and embraced what it calls being a great Leader.

To each one of them, those who are still present in life and those who are only in our memory...

Thank you very much!

Chapter 1

The Importance of Communication

- "The quality of our communication determines the quality of our relationships, and in the world of sales, those relationships are the cornerstone of success."
 — Dale Carnegie, *"How to win friends and influence people"*

Communication is the most powerful tool in the world of sales. It's not just about conveying information; it's about establishing a genuine connection with the customer. Effective communication builds trust, solves problems, and ultimately leads to positive outcomes. In this chapter, we'll delve into the key aspects of sales communication, exploring how it can improve customer relationships, build trust, and achieve effective conversions.

1.1 Definition of communication in sales

Communication in the field of sales goes beyond simple conversation. It is a process of exchanging information that involves words, gestures, attitudes, and above all, a deep ability to listen. The goal is to influence the customer's decision-making, ensuring that the message not only gets through, but is understood and accepted.

In sales, there are three fundamental components of communication:

1. **Verbal Communication**: What we say, how we say it and the tone we use.
2. **Non-Verbal Communication**: Gestures, postures, facial expressions, and everything that we transmit without words.
3. **Active Listening**: Understanding what the customer says and what they don't say, capturing their needs, desires, and fears.

1.2 The communication process: Elements and barriers

The sales communication process can be described as a sequence of steps:

1. **Sender**: The seller who wants to convey a message.
2. **Message**: The information you want to share, whether it's an offer, a solution, or an idea.
3. **Channel**: The medium through which the message is transmitted (e.g., in person, by phone, by email).
4. **Receiver**: The client who receives and interprets the message.
5. **Feedback**: The customer's response, which allows the salesperson to adjust their approach as needed.

Communication barriers:
Salespeople often face obstacles that make it difficult to communicate clearly and effectively. Some of these barriers include:

- **Environmental noise**: Physical or technological interruptions that distort the message.
- **Misperception**: When the customer interprets what is said incorrectly.
- **Lack of empathy**: Not connecting with the customer's emotional state.
- **Technical language**: Use of overly complicated terminology that the client does not understand.

1.3 Importance of active listening

Active **listening** is an essential skill in sales. It is not just about listening, but about showing a genuine interest in what the customer expresses. A study conducted by **Harvard Business Review** concluded that salespeople who practice active listening increase their conversion rates by 30%, as they are able to capture the customer's real needs and adapt their proposals accordingly.

Steps for effective active listening:
1. **Total concentration**: The salesperson must eliminate distractions and be fully present.
2. **Ask open-ended questions**: This allows you to learn more about the client's interests and concerns.
3. **Paraphrase and confirm**: Repeat what the customer has said to make sure it has been understood correctly.
4. **Read body language**: Many times, what is not said is just as important. Paying attention to nonverbal cues is key.

1.4 Verbal and non-verbal communication: Impact on sales

Verbal communication is what we say, but **nonverbal communication** (gestures, postures, expressions) has an even greater impact on how our message is perceived. According to researcher **Albert Mehrabian**, 55% of what we communicate comes from non-verbal cues, 38% from tone of voice, and only 7% from the content of words. This means that, in sales, how we say something can be more important than what we say.

Tips for good nonverbal communication:
- **Eye contact**: Maintaining eye contact builds trust.
- **Open posture**: Avoid crossing your arms or adopting a defensive posture.
- **Smile**: A genuine smile establishes an emotional connection.
- **Tone of voice**: Adjust the tone according to the context, using a calm and confident voice.

1.5 Communication and Trust-Building

Trust is the most important component in any business relationship, and this is built, in large part, through effective communication. According to a McKinsey study, 70% of purchasing decisions are based on how the customer perceives the relationship with the seller, rather than on the product or price.

This highlights the importance of establishing a strong relationship based on credibility and mutual respect.

Keys to building trust through communication:
1. **Transparency:** Being honest about what can be offered and the limits of the product or service.
2. **Empathy:** Showing that you understand the situation and the needs of the client.
3. **Consistency:** Be consistent in the message throughout all interactions.

Example:
A salesperson who listens to their customer's concerns, shows empathy for their situation, and offers realistic solutions builds a relationship of trust, often leading to recurring sales and recommendations.

1.6 Multichannel communication: Adapting to the customer

Nowadays, customers expect brands to communicate with them through different channels: emails, phone calls, online chats, social media, among others. The successful salesperson knows how to adapt his message and tone according to the medium.

Benefits of multichannel communication:
- **Flexibility:** The customer can choose the channel they are most comfortable with.
- **Expanded reach:** Allows the marketer to interact with a wider audience.
- **Personalization:** It's easier to tailor messaging to customer preferences and behaviors on each channel.

Conclusion

Effective **communication** is an art that, when mastered, can lead to consistent success in the world of sales. Understanding and practicing active listening, controlling verbal and non-verbal language, and building trust through transparency and empathy are all factors that differentiate an ordinary salesperson from an exceptional salesperson. In the next chapter, we'll explore how to break the ice in the first interactions with a customer, a crucial moment in establishing the initial connection.

Chapter 2

Personal Image and its Impact on Sales

- "In sales, the first impression is the most lasting. Your self-image speaks to your professionalism before you have a chance to do it yourself."

— Tom Peters, "The Brand You 50"

Personal image is one of the most influential elements in the sales process, as it affects the perception that customers have of the salesperson and, by extension, of the company and its products. In sales, the first impression is crucial and is often decisive in the success of a commercial interaction. This chapter delves into how self-image, including clothing, body language, and verbal communication, influences sales and how professionals can optimize these aspects to maximize their effectiveness. In addition, we will explore strategies to adapt the personal image to different contexts and audiences, ensuring that each interaction is aligned with the brand's objectives and customer expectations.

2.1 The importance of personal image in sales

Personal image encompasses not only physical appearance, but also the way a person presents, interacts, and communicates. In sales, this image is essential because it becomes the customer's first contact with the company and the product, directly influencing their perception and purchasing decisions.

2.1.1 First impressions and their influence

First impressions happen in a matter of seconds and have a lasting impact. Customers tend to form quick opinions about a salesperson based on factors such as clothing, body language, and tone of voice. These initial judgments can affect the customer's willingness to listen, trust, and engage with the salesperson.

- **Clothing**: The professional appearance conveys seriousness and confidence. A salesperson who dresses according to the environment and type of customer projects respect and professionalism.
- **Body language**: Posture, eye contact and gestures are elements that convey security and accessibility. Positive body language can facilitate emotional connection and improve communication.
- **Tone of voice and verbal expression**: The way of speaking, rhythm, and tone are essential to establish effective communication. A clear, firm tone projects confidence, while a leisurely pace shows patience and empathy.

2.1.2 Trust and credibility

A well-groomed personal image generates trust and credibility, essential factors to build lasting business relationships. When the customer perceives the salesperson as professional and confident, they are more likely to consider them an expert and trust their recommendations.

- **Authority projection**: The right personal image helps to project authority and dominance over the subject, making the client feel in the hands of an expert.
- **Brand cohesion**: The seller's personal image should align with the brand image. For example, in an innovative technology company, the salesperson can benefit from a modern and dynamic image that reflects the company's ethos.

2.2 Components of personal image in sales

The personal image is made up of several elements that, together, create a coherent and effective impression. Understanding and optimizing each of these elements can help sales professionals project an image that enhances their ability to influence and persuade.

2.2.1 Appearance and dress
Clothing is a fundamental aspect of personal image, as it is the first thing customers notice when interacting with a salesperson. It is important that the clothing is appropriate to the context and the type of client, adapting to the expectations of the environment in which they operate.

- **Formal dress code:** Formal suits and dresses project professionalism and are suitable for traditional business settings, such as financial or legal services.
- **Semi-formal dress code:** Jackets, shirts without ties, and formal pants are appropriate for less formal business environments, such as the technology sector.
- **Casual dress code:** In some creative industries or startups, casual and relaxed attire may be appropriate, as long as it reflects a sense of care and style.

2.2.2 Body language and nonverbal communication
Body language accounts for a large part of communication, and in sales, it's a deciding factor. This includes posture, eye contact, facial expression, and gestures, all of which must be aligned with the verbal message to convey coherence.

- **Open posture:** An open posture, with the shoulders relaxed and the hands visible, conveys accessibility and confidence.
- **Eye contact:** Looking into the customer's eyes naturally and continuously is essential to build trust. Proper eye contact suggests honesty and attention.
- **Smile:** A genuine smile facilitates the creation of a positive and close environment, helping to build a cordial relationship with the customer.
- **Gestures:** Gestures should be moderate and natural. Excessive gesticulations can be distracting or uncomfortable, while gentle gestures can help emphasize key points.

2.2.3 Verbal communication

The way you speak is as important as the content of the message. Clarity, tone, and pace all influence how the customer perceives the salesperson and the effectiveness of the message.

- **Clarity and precision**: Avoid the use of jargon or unnecessary technicalities that can confuse the customer. Expressing ideas clearly and accurately helps avoid misunderstandings.
- **Positive tone**: A positive and enthusiastic tone can generate interest and motivate the customer. It is important to adapt the tone to the customer's personality, always maintaining a professional attitude.
- **Active listening**: Listening carefully and responding to the client's questions and concerns demonstrates respect and a willingness to help.

2.3 Adaptation of personal image to different sales contexts

The sales context and the customer's profile influence the choice of the right personal image. The salesperson's ability to adjust their personal image based on the environment can improve the connection with the customer and increase the chances of success.

2.3.1 Sales in corporate environments

In formal corporate environments, such as the banking, legal, or financial sectors, personal image must project professionalism and competence. Formal dress is common and helps build credibility from the first contact.

- **Attire**: Full suit for men, and pantsuit or skirt for women. Neutral colors, such as navy, gray, or black, are preferable as they project authority.
- **Accessories**: They should be discreet and of good quality, such as watches and ties in sober tones. Jewelry should be minimal and elegant.
- **Body language**: Straight posture and firm eye contact. It is essential to avoid overly relaxed or casual behaviors.

2.3.2 Sales in creative sectors or startups

In more relaxed industries, such as technology, marketing, or the creative industries, personal image can be more casual and flexible. However, it is important to find a balance between comfort and professionalism.

- **Clothing**: Casual shirts, modern jackets, dark jeans and fashionable clothing, which project a current and reliable style. The appearance should reflect both creativity and professionalism.
- **Accessories**: Elements that provide a touch of individuality, such as designer glasses or a modern watch, can be well received in these environments.
- **Body language**: More relaxed and open posture, with a more casual approach. It is important to show authenticity and maintain accessible and friendly communication.

2.3.3 Sales to small businesses and SMEs

When selling to small and medium-sized businesses, the personal image should be approachable and friendly, projecting trust and a collaboration-oriented approach. Here, closeness and personalization are key to establishing a relationship of trust.

- **Attire**: A semi-formal approach, such as shirts and jackets, is appropriate. The colors can be a little more varied and less strict.
- **Accessories**: Few and discreet. It is important not to project an image that is too ostentatious that can disconnect with the customer.
- **Body language**: Close and expressive, with regular eye contact and gestures that convey empathy and understanding.

2.3.4 Sales in the health sector

Sales in the healthcare sector require an image that projects seriousness, confidence and professionalism. This is an industry where accuracy and ethics are essential, so the image must be impeccable.

- **Attire**: Formal, with specific suits or uniforms depending on the context. The use of light and neutral colors is common to reflect cleanliness and safety.
- **Accessories**: Minimal and practical, avoiding anything that could be distracting or seem inappropriate in a healthcare setting.
- **Body language**: Straight posture, smooth movements, and confident eye contact. It is important to project calm and tranquility to convey security to the customer.

2.4 Strategies for improvement and maintenance
A positive personal image in sales

Maintaining a consistent and positive personal image requires constant effort and attention to detail. The following strategies can help marketers optimize and sustain their personal image effectively.

2.4.1 Development of self-perception and self-confidence

An effective self-image starts with a **positive self-perception** and strong **self-confidence**. Salespeople who believe in their ability to deliver value to their customers project security and achieve a better connection.

- **Self-perception exercise**: Regularly assess one's strengths and weaknesses, and work on developing confidence-building skills.
- **Mental preparation before interactions**: Visualizing success before each meeting helps create a positive attitude and reduces nervousness.

2.4.2 Personal care and grooming

Self-care is essential to maintaining a polished and professional image. This aspect includes not only clothing, but also hygiene and general body care.

- **Personal hygiene**: Maintain good daily hygiene, including personal hygiene, hair care, and use of mild fragrances.
- **Skin and hair care**: Pay attention to the overall appearance, making sure the skin is clean, and the hair is well-groomed.
- **Physical health**: Maintaining good posture and energy helps to project an image of vitality and professionalism.

2.4.3 Ongoing Communication and Body Language Training

Ongoing **training** in communication and body language skills helps salespeople project a more effective image and respond appropriately to different contexts and types of customers.

- **Body language training**: Participate in workshops or courses that help perfect body language and interpret the client's nonverbal cues.
- **Active listening practice**: Learning how to respond effectively to customer needs through attentive listening and empathetic communication.
- **Regular feedback**: Soliciting feedback from colleagues and superiors on personal image and communication effectiveness helps identify areas for improvement.

2.4.4 Alignment with the company's brand and message

It is essential that the seller's personal image is in line with the **brand identity** and the **message that the company wants to convey**. Not only does this reinforce brand consistency, but it also helps create a more unified customer experience.

- **Understand the company's mission and vision**: Having a thorough understanding of the company's values and goals allows the salesperson to project a consistent image.
- **Brand-consistent attire and style**: Align dress and personal style with the brand's identity, whether it's traditional, innovative, or creative.

2.5 Personal Image Case Studies in different sales contexts

To understand how personal image can be adapted to different scenarios, let's look at some practical application examples.

2.5.1 Selling Financial Services to Corporations
- **Context**: The salesperson meets with CFOs of a multinational company to present an investment management solution.
- **Personal Image**: Dark suit, tie, professional briefcase and discreet luxury watches. Firm posture and constant eye contact. Accurate and straightforward communication.
- **Impact**: The projected image of trust and professionalism helps establish immediate credibility and facilitates serious conversation about investments.

2.5.2 Selling technology solutions in a startup
- **Context**: The salesperson presents innovative software to a development team at a technology startup.
- **Personal Image**: Modern jacket, dark jeans, and shirt without tie. Relaxed posture and use of open and friendly gestures.
- **Impact**: The more casual and modern appearance allows you to connect with a team that values creativity and flexibility, establishing an atmosphere of collaboration.

2.5.3 Selling products to an SME in the service sector
- **Context**: The salesperson visits a small service company to offer a package of products that will improve its operational efficiency.
- **Personal Image**: Semi-formal clothing, friendly colors and few accessories. Open and close posture, with empathetic communication.
- **Impact**: Approachable appearance and friendly attitude help build trust in an environment where closeness is valued, improving the likelihood of success.

Conclusion

Personal **image** is a powerful tool in a sales professional's arsenal. By paying attention to dress, body language, and verbal communication, and adapting to different contexts and types of customers, salespeople can significantly influence customer perception and increase their chances of success. Developing a personal image that inspires trust, and professionalism is essential to building strong and lasting relationships, establishing a solid foundation for success in the competitive world of sales.

Chapter 3

Body language in sales - the importance of greeting and non-verbal communication

- "Nonverbal body language can be more powerful than any verbal argument; your body is your first and most authentic salesman."
— Allan Pease, "Body Language"

Body **language** is a form of non-verbal communication that plays a critical role in the sales process. Often, customers form their first impressions based on nonverbal cues such as posture, eye contact, gestures, and particularly the initial greeting. In sales, greeting is a defining moment that sets the tone for interaction and can influence customer trust and comfort. This chapter explores in detail the importance of greeting, specifically the handshake, and how marketers can use body language strategically to maximize the impact of each interaction.

3.1 The importance of greeting in the sales process

The greeting is the first interaction between the salesperson and the customer, and it's crucial to establishing a positive connection. A proper greeting helps to create an environment of trust and mutual respect, two essential factors for effective communication and, therefore, for sales success.

3.1.1 First Impressions and the Power of Greeting

Research suggests that the first impression is formed in the first few seconds of an interaction. During this time, the client evaluates non-verbal aspects, such as posture, smiling, and, crucially, the handshake. An inappropriate or unprofessional greeting can make the customer feel uncomfortable or disinterested, while a well-executed greeting can foster a receptive and open attitude.

- **The greeting as a first contact**: In sales, the greeting is not only a gesture of courtesy, but an opportunity to project confidence and professionalism.
- **The perception of competence**: A firm and friendly greeting can make the customer perceive the salesperson as a confident and competent person, which increases credibility from the beginning of the interaction.

3.1.2 The handshake as a connecting tool

The **handshake** is one of the most universal and meaningful gestures in body language. It represents a tacit agreement of respect and goodwill and can influence the customer's perception of the seller. The handshake is an opportunity to establish brief **physical contact** that can facilitate the construction of a closer relationship.

- **The firmness of the handshake**: A handshake that is too strong may seem aggressive, while one that is too weak may indicate a lack of interest or insecurity. It's important to find a balance that conveys confidence without making the customer uncomfortable.
- **Duration**: A handshake should be brief, between 2 and 3 seconds. Excessive duration can be uncomfortable and perceived as an invasion of personal space.
- **Eye contact and smile**: It is essential to accompany the handshake with proper eye contact and a genuine smile, as this complements the gesture and helps to create a positive impression.

3.2 Handshake Positions and Their Meaning

The handshake can take different forms and positions, each of which communicates something different. It is important for salespeople to understand these nuances in order to project the desired image and adapt to the customer.

3.2.1 Neutral Handshake
The **neutral handshake** is the most common type and is performed with the palms vertically and fingers closed, in firm but not tight contact. This position conveys equality and mutual respect, making it the best choice for most sales interactions.

- **When to use it**: It is appropriate in all professional situations, as it projects balance and neutrality.
- **Interpretation**: Communicates a disposition of respect, without trying to dominate or submit. It is ideal for establishing a foundation of egalitarian communication.

3.2.2 Dominant handshake
The **dominant handshake** is characterized by a slight downward tilt of the salesperson's palm, forcing the customer's palm to be up. This gesture can project a position of authority or control.

- **When to use it**: In situations where it is required to demonstrate authority or when seeking to reinforce leadership, but it should be used sparingly.
- **Interpretation**: Communicates an attitude of dominance and control. It can be useful for projecting firmness, but if used excessively or without considering the context, it can be perceived as aggressive or authoritarian.

3.2.3 Submissive Handshake
In the **submissive handshake**, the salesperson's palm is slightly tilted upwards, allowing the customer to have their hand in a dominant position. This gesture can convey willingness to collaborate and respect for the customer.

- **When to use it**: In situations where it is necessary to soften authority or create an atmosphere of support and understanding, such as when handling complaints or trying to recover the relationship with an unhappy customer.
- **Interpretation**: It projects an attitude of openness and submission. It can help reduce tensions and establish a more empathetic relationship, but too much can suggest weakness.

3.2.4 Handshake with both hands (diplomatic handshake)

The **diplomatic squeeze** is performed by placing one hand on the client's hand while giving the squeeze with the other. This gesture suggests warmth and familiarity and can be helpful in creating a deeper connection.

- **When to use it**: It is suitable in contexts where you want to strengthen a relationship of trust, especially when there is already a previous relationship with the customer. However, it should be avoided in the first few meetings, as it can be too intimate.
- **Interpretation**: It communicates empathy and closeness, but it can be perceived as invasive if used excessively or in overly formal relationships.

3.2.5 Arm handshake

The **arm handshake** involves a normal handshake accompanied by a light pat on the client's forearm or shoulder. This gesture is common in contexts where there is already a close and trusting relationship.

- **When to use it**: It is appropriate for more informal and family interactions, where camaraderie and affection are sought.
- **Interpretation**: It transmits a close and trusting relationship. However, if it is used in overly formal contexts or with people who do not know the seller well, it may seem too familiar.

3.3 Other aspects of body language in greeting

In addition to the handshake, other aspects of body language in greeting also play an important role in how the salesperson is perceived. These include eye contact, smiling, and overall posture.

3.3.1 Eye Contact

Proper **eye contact** is essential to establishing a genuine connection with the customer. Avoiding eye contact can be interpreted as a lack of confidence or interest, while excessive eye contact can seem intimidating.

- **Duration**: Look directly into the customer's eyes during the handshake and maintain eye contact for a few seconds. It is essential not to prolong the contact too much to avoid discomfort.
- **Frequency**: Throughout the conversation, eye contact should be regular but natural. Making eye contact at the end of each sentence reinforces interest and attention.

3.3.2 Smile

Smiling is one of the most powerful nonverbal gestures. A genuine smile conveys kindness and willingness to help, making it easier to create a positive and welcoming environment.

- **Naturalness**: The smile must be natural and not forced. A genuine smile involves both the mouth and the eyes, and projects an authentic and friendly attitude.
- **Temporality**: Smiling at the beginning and during the conversation, especially when the customer shares something positive. It is also useful for smoothing out tense situations.

3.3.3 Posture and personal distance

Posture and **personal distance** are essential to convey respect and accessibility. An open posture and proper distance when greeting is essential to making a good first impression.

- **Open posture**: Maintain an upright posture, with your shoulders relaxed and without crossing your arms. These projects trust and openness.
- **Personal distance**: Respect the customer's personal space. The ideal distance for a greeting is about an outstretched arm. Invading personal space can make the customer feel uncomfortable.

3.4 Adapting greeting and body language to different cultural contexts

Body language, and particularly the handshake, varies considerably between different cultures. It is essential for salespeople to adapt their greeting and body language to the customer's cultural context to avoid misunderstandings and show respect for their customs.

3.4.1 Handshake in Western Cultures

In Western cultures, such as the United States and Europe, the handshake is the most common greeting in business contexts. The firmness of the squeeze is important, as too weak a squeeze can be interpreted as a lack of interest or insecurity.

3.4.2 Handshake in Asian cultures

In many Asian countries, the handshake is less common and may be accompanied by a slight bow. The firmness of the grip is usually softer than in Western cultures, and prolonged eye contact can be perceived as disrespectful.

- **Japan**: It is common to bow slightly instead of a handshake, or to combine both. Handshakes are usually soft, and eye contact is maintained briefly.
- **China**: The handshake is light and may be accompanied by a slight bow. Eye contact is brief, and showing a lot of emotion can be considered inappropriate.

3.4.3 Alternatives to the Handshake in Middle Eastern Cultures

In some Middle Eastern cultures, handshakes between people of different genders may not be appropriate due to cultural norms. In these cases, it is better to follow the customer's lead. In some places, a verbal greeting or a slight bow of the head are suitable options.

3.5 Practical examples of greeting in different sales contexts

3.5.1 Greeting at a Corporate Business Meeting

Context: A salesperson meets a potential customer at a financial services company.

- **Handshake**: Neutral and firm, accompanied by direct eye contact and a slight smile.
- **Impact**: It projects professionalism and security, which is essential in the formal context of financial services.

3.5.2 Greeting at an International Trade Show

Context: A salesperson greets a customer from an Asian country at a trade show in Japan.

- **Handshake**: Gentle and brief, combined with a slight tilt of the head and moderate eye contact.
- **Impact**: Show respect for local customs and help establish a good relationship of trust from the start.

3.5.3 Greeting at a product presentation at a tech startup

Context: A salesperson greets a young, multicultural development team at a tech startup.

- **Handshake**: Firm but casual, accompanied by a wide smile and friendly eye contact. The posture is relaxed, and a slight distance is maintained to respect personal space.
- **Impact**: The combination of firmness and accessibility projects a reliable and adaptable image, which resonates well in an informal and dynamic work environment.

Conclusion

Greeting **and body language** are crucial aspects of personal image in sales, significantly influencing how the salesperson is perceived from the first moment. By mastering different handshake styles and adapting body language to different contexts and cultures, salespeople can create stronger connections, establish trust, and optimize every interaction. The key is to understand the power of nonverbal cues and use them strategically to project an image of professionalism and accessibility that fosters success in the sales process.

Chapter 4

How the personality of individuals influences the sales process

- "Sales is a process of understanding people, and that means understanding their personalities and what drives their decisions."
— *Daniel H. Pink, "To Sell Is Human"*

Every sales interaction is influenced by one essential factor: **personality**. Both the seller and the customer play a key role in the way communication develops and, ultimately, in the success of the transaction. Understanding personality types, how they relate to each other, and how to tailor the sales approach to the customer's particularities is critical to maximizing opportunities for success. This chapter explores in depth how personalities influence the sales process, how to detect personality types, and adapt sales strategies to each.

4.1 What is personality and why is it important in sales?

Personality is defined as the set of characteristics, behaviors, and attitudes that define a person and the way they interact with the world. In sales, personality influences the way people make decisions, communicate, and build relationships. The salesperson's ability to understand and adjust to the customer's personality can significantly increase the odds of success.

Key factors about the influence of personality on sales:
1. **Communication and empathy**: Different personalities require different communication styles. Some clients are more analytical, while others respond better to an emotional approach.
2. **Decision-making**: The customer's personality affects how they make decisions. Some need time to reflect, while others act more impulsively.
3. **Relationship building**: The personal connection between the salesperson and the customer depends on how their personalities interact. The salesperson who adjusts their style to align with the customer generates more trust and affinity.

4.2 Personality Models and Customer Types

There are multiple models that categorize personalities into types. One of the best known in sales is the **DISC Model**, which classifies personalities into four large categories: **Dominant (D), Influential (I), Stable (S) and Conscientious (C)**. This model allows salespeople to tailor their communication style and approach based on the customer's dominant personality.

4.2.1 The DISC model
1. **Dominant (D)**
   Clients with dominant personalities are straightforward, results oriented, and enjoy being in control. They prefer meetings to be quick and concise, and they are not comfortable with beating around the bush or indecision.

Key features:
- Focused on goals and results.
- They make quick decisions.
- They like control and independence.

How to approach them in sales:
- Be direct and specific. Present the benefits clearly and focus on tangible results.

- Avoid wasting time on unnecessary details, as these customers value efficiency.
- Give them options and keep the conversation goal oriented.

2. **Influential (I)**

Influential customers are outgoing, expressive, and tend to make decisions based on emotions and social interaction. They enjoy conversations and interpersonal relationships. This type of customer values personal connection and positive experiences.

Key features:
- Highly sociable and charismatic.
- Focused on personal interaction and emotion.
- They prefer a positive and relaxed atmosphere.

How to approach them in sales:
- Establish a personal relationship before moving on to the technical details.
- Be enthusiastic and emotional, highlighting the benefits on a personal or emotional level.
- Offer testimonials from other customers or success stories that they can relate to them.

3. **Stable(s)**

Customers with stable personalities are patient, reliable, and seek security. They prefer a calm approach and seek long-term relationships based on trust. This personality type tends to be more reserved and avoid conflict.

Key features:
- Patient and reflective.
- They value stability and security.
- They are looking for long-term relationships.

How to approach them in sales:
- Provide enough time for them to reflect before planning.
- Create an environment of trust and be sure to address any concerns or concerns they may have.
- Avoid pressing them. Make sure they feel comfortable and confident with the process.

4. **Conscientious (C)**
   Conscientious clients are detail-oriented, analytical, and focus on accuracy and logic. They value well-structured information and like to review all the details before making decisions.

Key features:
- Highly analytical and accurate.
- They focus on data and facts.
- They are cautious and methodical when making decisions.

How to approach them in sales:
- It provides technical details, reports, and analysis. These customers prefer a data-driven approach.
- Be precise and avoid generalizations or assumptions.
- Give them time to analyze the information before making a decision.

4.3 How to identify the customer's personality

Identifying the customer's personality from the beginning of the interaction can allow the salesperson to adapt their strategy effectively. There are several signals that can help salespeople classify customers into one of the DISC types. These cues include both verbal and nonverbal language.

4.3.1 Verbal cues
- **Dominant (D) customers** tend to use phrases like, "I want quick results" or "How long will this take?" They focus on the outcome and quick decisions.
- **Influential customers often** mention other people and personal experiences: "My colleagues would be interested too" or "I'd love to hear what others think about this."
- **Stable Clients (S)** often express concern about stability and relationships: "I'd like to think about this a little more" or "What kind of ongoing support do you offer?"
- **Conscientious customers (C)** ask specific, detailed questions: "Do you have a report with the technical specifications?" or "I'd like to see the full data before making a decision."

4.3.2 Nonverbal cues
- **Dominant (D) clients** often display controlling body language, with confident postures and rapid movements.
- **Influential customers** tend to be more expressive with their gestures, making constant eye contact and smiling frequently.

- **Stable Clients (S)** are characterized by a relaxed posture and can move slowly, reflecting patience and tranquility.
- **Conscientious customers (C)** tend to seem more reserved, maintain an attentive posture and tend to analyze details with their eyes, observing every aspect of the conversation.

4.4 Adapt the sales approach according to personality type

Once the customer's personality type has been identified, the next step is to adjust the sales strategy to align with their preferences. Below are detailed strategies for each personality type.

4.4.1 Strategy for Dominant Customers (D)
- **Be concise and direct**: Dominant customers don't have time for lengthy explanations. Answer their questions quickly and focus on the core benefits.
- **Provide options**: These customers like to feel like they're in control. Providing them with several options and letting them decide which one is best for them will increase the chances of success.
- **Show tangible results**: These customers want to know how your product or service will directly benefit them. Use metrics, success stories, and other measurable results.

4.4.2 Strategy for Influencers (I)
- **Create a positive experience**: Excitement and enthusiasm are important for influential customers. It generates an environment of positive energy and optimism.
- **Use stories**: Influential customers respond well to success stories and testimonials from other people. Tell them how your product has helped others in a similar situation.
- **Make a personal connection**: Influential customers enjoy social relationships. Spend time talking about common interests and building a relationship beyond the sale.

4.4.3 Strategy for Stable Customers (S)
- **Be patient and considerate**: Don't pressure these customers. Give them the time they need to make a decision and make sure they feel comfortable during the process.
- **Provides security**: Stable customers value trust and reliability. Highlight the ongoing support and long-term relationship they may have with you and your company.

- **Be clear and reassuring**: Make sure they understand all aspects of the transaction and address any concerns they may have.

4.4.4 Strategy for Conscientious Clients (C)
- **Provides detailed insights**: Conscientious customers need to see all the data before deciding. Provide them with detailed analysis, reports, and specifications.
- **Be precise**: Avoid generalities. These customers value accuracy and clarity, so you should be specific in your answers and in the information you provide.
- **Offer comparisons**: Conscientious customers often want to compare different options before making a decision. Offers comparative analysis to help them evaluate options.

4.5 The seller's personality and its impact

Just as the customer's personality influences the sales process, the salesperson's personality also plays a crucial role. Some salespeople are naturally more outgoing, while others are more analytical or empathetic. Self-awareness is key for salespeople to use their strengths effectively and recognize when they need to adjust their style to suit different types of customers.

4.5.1 Extroverted and Introverted Salespeople
- **Extroverted salespeople**: These salespeople are usually more expressive and enjoy social interactions. They perform well with influential and dominant customers as they can match their energy level and enthusiasm. However, they must be careful not to overwhelm stable or conscientious customers with too much information or emotion.
- **Introverted Salespeople**: Introverted salespeople tend to be more thoughtful and calmer. They can build deep, trusting relationships with stable, conscientious clients, who value accuracy and thoughtfulness. However, they should strive to be more energetic and expressive when interacting with dominant or influential customers.

4.5.2 Adaptation of the seller's personality
A good salesperson is able to adapt his style according to the situation. For example, an extroverted salesperson working with a conscientious customer should focus on providing data and be less emotional. On the other hand, an introverted salesperson may need to put in more effort to generate excitement when working with an influential customer.

Conclusion

Understanding how personalities influence the sales process is a key component for any salesperson looking to improve their effectiveness. The ability to identify the customer's personality type and adjust the sales approach according to their preferences not only increases the odds of success, but also builds stronger, longer-lasting relationships.

Chapter 5

Psychology of human behavior applied to sales

- "Purchasing decisions are deeply influenced by emotions and not just logic; Understanding this psychology is essential for any marketer."
  — *Robert B. Cialdini, "Influence: The Psychology of Persuasion"*

The **psychology of human behavior** is a discipline that studies the motivations, emotions, thought processes, and actions that people perform consciously and unconsciously. Applied to sales, this branch of psychology becomes a fundamental tool to understand customers' purchase motivations, the way they make decisions, and how emotions and perceptions influence the buying process. In this chapter, we'll delve into the psychology of human behavior and its relevance to sales professionals, addressing key psychological theories, emotional and cognitive factors that affect purchasing decisions, and how to use this knowledge to close more sales effectively.

5.1 The psychology of purchasing decisions

Every purchase decision is influenced by a combination of **rational factors** and **emotional factors**. While many customers believe they make decisions logically, much of the buying process is deeply ingrained in the **emotional unconscious**. The effective salesperson understands this duality and learns to touch the right buttons to influence both areas.

5.1.1 Emotional factors

The human brain makes decisions based, in large part, on emotions. Psychologist Daniel Kahneman, in his work *Thinking Fast, Thinking Slow*, argues that humans act primarily through two systems of thought: the **fast system** (intuitive and emotional) and the **slow system** (analytical and rational). In sales, the fast system is frequently dominant, as customers often react emotionally before justifying their decision with logic.

Main emotions that influence purchases:
1. **Desire and aspiration**: Many purchases are driven by the desire to achieve a goal or status. Products that promise to improve a person's life, whether emotionally or physically, often arouse strong impulses to buy.
2. **Fear of Losing: Scarcity** or **urgency** are powerful tools that play on the fear of missing out on an opportunity. This can be a limited-time offer or a limited amount of stock.
3. **Trust**: Customers tend to buy more when they trust the brand, seller, or product. Building trust and security reduces emotional barriers to engagement.
4. **Identification**: Consumers want to see themselves reflected in the product or brand. When they feel that something is aligned with their identity or values, they are more likely to buy it.

5.1.2 Cognitive factors

Although emotions play a crucial role, cognitive factors are also determinants in the purchasing decision-making process. These are those elements that the rational brain takes into account to justify a decision.

Most common cognitive factors in purchasing decisions:
1. **Cost-benefit**: Customers are constantly evaluating whether the perceived value of a product justifies its cost. This is where price comparisons, perceived quality, and product features come into play.
2. **Relevance**: The customer needs to perceive that the product or service satisfies a specific need. Alignment between customer needs and supply is essential.

3. **Product confidence**: The perception that a product is reliable and effective is crucial. Customers are looking for tangible evidence such as reviews, testimonials, case studies, or performance statistics.
4. **Ease of use**: A product that seems complicated or difficult to use can lead to doubts. Customers are looking for simplicity and clarity in how the product or service will benefit them.

5.2 Consumer behavior: Key psychological theories

Understanding the psychology behind purchasing decisions involves becoming familiar with several key theories of human behavior. These theories provide us with a framework for interpreting how and why customers act the way they do in a sales situation.

5.2.1 Maslow's theory and the pyramid of needs

Abraham Maslow developed the **Hierarchy of Needs Theory** to explain how human motivations vary depending on the satisfaction of basic needs. Maslow's pyramid consists of five levels of needs, ranging from the most basic to the most complex:

1. **Physiological needs**: Food, water, shelter. Purchases aimed at satisfying these needs are essential, such as basic necessities.
2. **Security**: Physical and economic protection. This is where products such as insurance, security systems, and financial services come into play.
3. **Affiliation and love**: People want to belong to groups and be accepted. Products such as clothing, branded products, social media, and group experiences are designed to meet this need.
4. **Recognition**: People desire respect and status. Luxury products or premium services are examples of how brands can take advantage of this motivation.
5. **Self-realization**: The need for personal development and full fulfillment. This level is associated with products or services that improve skills, promote creativity or encourage personal growth.

The salesperson who can identify which level of the pyramid their customer is at will be able to tailor their sales strategy to meet those specific needs.

5.2.2 Skinner's theory of reinforcement

Psychologist B.F. Skinner proposed the **Reinforcement Theory**, which posits that behaviors can be modified through rewards or punishments. In sales, this translates into the ability to **reinforce** the customer's buying behavior through incentives or tangible benefits.

- **Positive reinforcement**: Offering discounts, bonuses, additional products, or any other type of reward can incentivize customers to make purchasing decisions faster.
- **Negative reinforcement**: Although the term sounds negative, negative reinforcement simply means removing something undesirable. For example, ensuring a hassle-free return process or eliminating financial risk for the customer.

5.2.3 Cialdini's theory of persuasion

Professor Robert Cialdini developed the **Theory of Persuasion**, which details six key principles that can be effectively applied in sales to influence customer decision-making:

1. **Reciprocity**: People feel the need to return favors. If a salesperson offers something of value without asking for anything in return (such as a free sample or valuable information), the customer will be inclined to reciprocate.
2. **Commitment and consistency**: Customers tend to be consistent with their previous commitments. Once a customer expresses interest or takes a small action, they're more likely to complete the purchase.
3. **Social approval**: People tend to follow the behavior of others, especially when they are undecided. Displaying testimonials, reviews, and the popularity of a product can increase the likelihood of a sale.
4. **Authority**: People trust experts or authority figures. Endorsing products with expert testimony or reliable data bolsters credibility.
5. **Sympathy**: People prefer to buy from people they like. Developing warm and friendly relationships with customers is crucial.
6. **Scarcity**: People value more what is limited or difficult to obtain. Urgency and limited supply are powerful tools in sales.

5.3 The influence of cognitive biases on sales

Human beings do not always make rational decisions. Often, our decisions are influenced by **cognitive biases**, which are mental shortcuts that help us process information quickly but can also lead us to make irrational decisions. In the context of sales, understanding and leveraging these biases can help salespeople influence customer decisions.

5.3.1 Anchoring bias

Anchoring **bias** occurs when people rely too much on the first piece of information they receive (the "anchor") when making decisions. In sales, anchoring can be used when initially presenting a higher price or advanced features of a product, causing the customer to mentally compare all subsequent offerings to that initial anchor.

Example: A car salesman may present the luxury model first before showing the most affordable options. By doing this, the customer will tend to see the cheaper options as a better deal compared to the price of the luxury car.

5.3.2 Bandwagon effect

This bias refers to the tendency of people to follow the actions or decisions of the majority. People often feel more comfortable making decisions that others have previously made.

Example: Showing the customer that the product you are offering is the best seller or most popular in the market can influence them to follow the crowd and make the purchase.

5.3.3 Confirmation bias

Confirmation **bias** is the tendency to seek out or interpret information that confirms our pre-existing beliefs. A salesperson can use this bias by identifying the customer's beliefs or assumptions and reinforcing them throughout the presentation of the product or service.

Example: If a customer believes that one type of product is the best, the salesperson can focus his argument on highlighting the characteristics of that product, confirming the customer's opinion.

5.4 Emotional selling

In a world where brands and products are plentiful, emotions play an even bigger role. **Emotional selling** is about creating a strong emotional connection between the customer and the product or service. Not only does this approach help close sales, but it also builds long-term loyalty.

5.4.1 Creating Stories

Stories are a powerful tool in sales, as they connect emotionally with customers and allow them to imagine how the product could improve their lives. Telling a story about how the product solved another customer's problem can be more effective than simply listing features.

Example: An insurance salesperson might tell the story of a family that benefited from life insurance during a difficult time, rather than just describing the terms of the policy.

5.4.2 Generate positive expectations

People make decisions based on their emotional expectations about the future. An effective salesperson knows how to generate positive expectations by showing the customer how their life will improve after purchasing the product or service.

Example: A sales consultant can talk about how using the software will improve the client's productivity and allow them to have more free time for their hobbies or family.

5.5 Sales psychology case studies

Case 1: Selling a Travel Package

Context: A client is looking for a luxury vacation package but is undecided. The seller uses principles of **scarcity** and **authority**, highlighting that there are few places available and showing reviews from recognized travel influencers.

Result: The customer feels an immediate urgency to make a decision and chooses to book the vacation package.

Case 2: Selling business software

Context: An entrepreneur is evaluating software options for their company but hesitates whether the investment is worth it. The seller applies the **anchoring bias**, starting with a more expensive product and then offering a more affordable option. It also uses the principle of **reciprocity**, offering a free product demonstration.

Result: The entrepreneur perceives the affordable offer as a valuable opportunity and decides to make the purchase.

Conclusion

Knowledge of the psychology of human behavior is a critical tool in any successful salesperson's arsenal. Understanding how customers make decisions, what emotional and cognitive factors drive them, and how to positively influence their thought processes allows salespeople to not only close more sales, but also create lasting, trusting relationships with their customers.

Chapter 6

Definition and types of customers

- "A customer is someone we must serve, care for, and keep satisfied. Their loyalty is the result of every interaction they have with us."
  — *Jeffrey Gitomer, "Little Red Book of Selling"*

Knowing customers in depth and understanding their different typologies is essential to develop successful sales strategies. Every customer has specific motivations, needs, and behaviors, and recognizing these differences can make the difference between a successful sale and a missed opportunity. In this chapter, we'll explore in depth the **definition of the different types of customers**, their characteristics, and how to develop specific approaches for each. We will also look at how customer segmentation allows companies to maximize their impact on the market, better adapting to consumer demands and offering a personalized experience that strengthens the relationship with the brand.

6.1 What is a customer: Definition and essential elements

In the context of sales, a **customer** is any person, company, or organization that purchases products or services from a supplier. But the definition goes beyond a simple transaction. A customer is a critical asset that, throughout its lifecycle, contributes to a company's profitability and success. The modern sales approach recognizes the customer as the center of business strategy, which means that every interaction, process, and product must be designed to meet their expectations and create a long-term relationship.

6.1.1 Importance of knowing the customer

Understanding who the customer is, is the foundation of an effective sales strategy. This involves more than knowing their demographic profile; It also requires understanding their **behaviors**, preferences, values, **and** purchase motivations. By recognizing the unique characteristics of each customer, you can adjust your message, channel, and offer in a way that makes it more engaging and relevant.

6.1.2 Internal Customer and External Customer

Most sales strategies focus on the **external customer** – the person or entity that buys products or services from the company. However, it is also essential to consider the **internal customer**, which refers to the employees and departments within the organization that are a fundamental part of the process of delivering value to the external customer.

- **External Customer**: Person or entity outside the organization that acquires the products or services. This customer requires personalized attention and approach to achieve their satisfaction and loyalty.
- **Internal Customer**: Includes all employees, departments and collaborators who are involved in the value creation process. Keeping internal customers satisfied improves operational efficiency and contributes to a better external customer experience.

6.2 Classification of customers according to your buying behavior

One of the most common approaches to categorizing customers is according to their **buying behavior**, which provides insights into how they interact with the company and what factors influence their purchase decision. This classification allows you to design sales strategies that best suit each profile.

6.2.1 Prospective customer

The prospective customer is someone who has shown interest in the product or service, but has not yet made the purchase decision. This is the first step of the sales cycle, and while it doesn't generate immediate revenue, it represents an opportunity to attract a new customer.

- **Characteristics**: It is in the research and comparison phase. You may have requested information, downloaded a catalog, or visited the company's website.
- **Strategy**: The focus should be on **customer education** and **nutrition**. Offering useful and relevant content, such as guides, webinars, and testimonials, helps convert the prospect into a lead.

6.2.2 New Customer

The new customer is the one who has made their first purchase. This is a crucial time to strengthen the relationship, as first impressions have a lasting impact on the customer's perception of the company.

- **Features**: You have recently purchased and are evaluating the experience of your first purchase. He does not yet have loyalty to the brand.
- **Strategy**: Focus efforts on providing excellent **after-sales experience** and **close follow-up** to resolve any questions or inconveniences. Incentivizing future purchases through discounts or welcome programs can help turn the new customer into a returning customer.

6.2.3 Repeat customer

A regular customer is one who has made several purchases and has begun to develop a relationship with the brand. These customers are critical, as they consistently contribute to the company's revenue.

- **Characteristics**: Buys periodically, is familiar with the company's offer and has clear expectations.
- **Strategy**: Implement **loyalty** and **rewards** programs that reinforce customer loyalty. It is important to maintain continuous and personalized communication to ensure that the regular customer feels valued and continues to buy.

6.2.4 Loyal customer

The loyal customer is one of the most valuable assets for a business, as they not only buy repeatedly, but also promote the brand and recommend products or services to others.

- **Features**: High brand satisfaction, actively recommends, and less price sensitive.
- **Strategy**: Create exclusive programs and offer additional benefits, such as **early access to new products, invitations to events**, or **special discounts**. Exclusive communication channels can also be established for this type of customer, thus reinforcing their feeling of belonging and appreciation.

6.2.5 Dissatisfied Customer

The dissatisfied customer has had a negative experience and is at risk of not buying again. Although this type of customer presents challenges, it also represents an opportunity to learn and improve.

- **Characteristics**: You have expressed your dissatisfaction through complaints or refund requests. You are at risk of leaving the brand and sharing your negative experience with others.
- **Strategy**: Address dissatisfaction proactively, listening to their concerns and offering quick solutions. Compensation, if appropriate, can help win back the customer and, in some cases, turn them into a brand advocate by showing them that their opinion is valued.

6.2.6 Occasional Customer

The occasional customer makes sporadic purchases and does not have a stable buying pattern. Although this customer does not generate recurring revenue, it represents an opportunity to increase the frequency of their purchases.

- **Features**: Shop from time to time, without clear brand loyalty.
- **Strategy**: Encourage recurrence through **specific promotions, personalized reminders** or **exclusive offers**. Creating a memorable shopping experience can help turn the casual customer into a repeat customer.

6.3 Customer segmentation according to the customer lifecycle

The **customer life cycle** refers to the different stages that a customer goes through in their relationship with a company. Each stage requires a distinct approach to maximize customer satisfaction and value.

6.3.1 Lead

The lead is the person who has shown interest but has not yet become a customer. This phase is essential for building a strong customer base through **recruitment** and **nurturing techniques**.

- **Characteristics**: You have expressed interest, but have not made any purchases.
- **Strategy**: Convert the prospect into a customer through **content marketing strategies, email marketing,** and **trial offers**. The goal is to bring the lead to the consideration phase through a relevant offer tailored to their needs.

6.3.2 New Customer

The new customer represents an opportunity to build a strong relationship from the start. In this phase, the company must ensure that the shopping experience is satisfactory and that the customer receives all the necessary support.

- **Characteristics**: You have made your first purchase and are evaluating the experience.
- **Strategy**: Closely **monitor** and provide **excellent after-sales support**. In addition, the new customer can benefit from a **welcome program** that explains the advantages of being a customer and offers discounts or complementary products.

6.3.3 Returning Customer

The recurring customer is the one who makes purchases frequently. He has moved from the initial phase and is comfortable with the brand, making him a stable source of income for the company.

- **Features**: Buys regularly and has defined expectations.
- **Strategy**: Implement **loyalty** and **rewards programs** to strengthen your relationship with the brand. Offering **exclusive products** or **personalization** can enhance your experience and strengthen your loyalty.

6.3.4 Sleeping Client

The sleeping customer is someone who has stopped interacting with the company, but who can still be recovered through a reactivation strategy.

- **Features**: You have recently stopped making purchases, but you have a history with the company.
- **Strategy**: Use **reactivation campaigns** with **personalized offers** or **reminders** to motivate the customer to resume their relationship with the brand. Often, an **incentive** or a **new offer** can pique the customer's interest.

6.3.5 Lost Customer

The lost customer has decided not to buy again and has possibly switched to the competition. Despite this, it's helpful to understand why the customer has been lost and take steps to prevent other customers from following the same path.

- **Features**: You have not made purchases in a long time and have decided not to return.
- **Strategy**: Analyze the reasons for their departure through **surveys** or **follow-up calls**. If possible, try a reactivation strategy or learn from experience to improve the service and avoid future losses.

6.4 Ranking Customers Based on Their Value to the Business

Customer **value** to the business can vary considerably, from those that bring in significant revenue on a recurring basis to those that only generate sporadic profits. Understanding this aspect allows you to focus resources and strategies on the most profitable segments.

6.4.1 Premium Client

The premium customer represents those who make high-value purchases on a regular basis. They are critical to the company's profitability and generally show significant brand loyalty.

- **Features**: High purchase frequency and large spending volumes. His relationship with the company is ongoing and valuable.
- **Strategy**: Offer **exclusive experiences** and **personalized attention**. This customer expects differential treatment that reinforces their status and makes them feel valued. VIP programs and unique discounts are effective strategies to retain this type of customer.

6.4.2 Profitable Customer

The profitable customer generates constant revenue and represents a valuable component to the business, even if it does not have the impact of a premium customer. However, they are profitable enough to justify loyalty efforts.

- **Features**: Make consistent purchases, although not of high value. It brings stable and long-term profits.
- **Strategy**: Offer **exclusive benefits** on a regular basis and maintain **constant communication**. Incentives such as occasional discounts or complementary products can strengthen their loyalty and ensure their continuity.

6.4.3 Low-value customer

The low-value customer makes occasional, low-volume purchases. Although they are not profitable on their own, they can represent an opportunity if you can increase your purchase frequency or your average ticket value.

- **Features**: Sporadic and low-cost purchase. It has a limited relationship with the brand.
- **Strategy**: Implement **upselling** and **cross-selling** strategies to increase the value of your purchases. In some cases, it may be more cost-effective to prioritize other segments, but this type of customer can become a profitable customer if properly incentivized.

6.5 Psychological characteristics of clients

In addition to demographic and behavioral aspects, customers can also be classified according to their **psychological characteristics**, which includes their **personality, attitudes, values,** and **preferences**. This analysis allows salespeople to connect on a deeper level with the customer, adapting their tactics and messages according to the psychological tendencies of each profile.

6.5.1 Rational and emotional customers
- **Rational customers**: They prioritize facts, data, and detailed information. Their buying process tends to be analytical and meticulous.
    - **Strategy**: Provide **hard data, benchmarking,** and **value testing** that highlights the tangible benefits of the product.
- **Emotional customers**: They are driven by their emotions and are more interested in how the product makes them feel or how it will improve their lives.
    - **Strategy**: Use **stories, experiences,** and **testimonials** that connect emotionally with the client. Focus on the positives and how the product or service will impact your life.

6.5.2 Innovative and conservative customers
- **Innovative customers**: They are open to new ideas and are looking for cutting-edge products. They value novelty and exclusivity.
    - **Strategy**: Highlight **the unique** and **differential aspects** of the product, and offer opportunities for **early access** or **exclusivity**.
- **Conservative customers**: They prefer traditional and reliable products. They are more cautious when making decisions and tend to stick to what they know.

- **Strategy**: Emphasize the **reliability** and **safety** of the product. Providing proof of their effectiveness and success in the marketplace can boost their confidence.

6.6 Case studies:
Strategies adapted to customer types

Case 1: Strategy for a premium customer in a luxury clothing store
- **Context**: Premium customer who regularly visits the store and spends a considerable amount on each purchase.
- **Strategy**: Offer **personalized services**, such as a **personal shopper, exclusive discounts**, and **early access** to new collections. This strategy reinforces their feeling of exclusivity and loyalty to the brand.

Case 2: Reactivating a Sleeping Customer on a Streaming Platform
- **Context**: Customer who has unsubscribed from the platform after one year of active use.
- **Strategy**: Send an **email campaign** with a **special reactivation offer** that includes a discount or an extended trial period. The goal is to remind the customer of the benefits of the service and motivate their return.

Case 3: Increasing the frequency of purchase of an occasional customer in an electronics store
- **Context**: Customer who makes small purchases sporadically.
- **Strategy**: Use **specific promotions** and **personalized reminders** to incentivize purchases. The goal is to create a **memorable shopping experience** that motivates brand loyalty.

Conclusion

Knowing and segmenting customers according to their characteristics and behaviors allows companies to develop more effective and personalized sales strategies. Each type of customer, from the new to the premium customer, has their own expectations and motivations, and adapting to them can make a big difference in the long-term relationship. A deep understanding of customer types and their needs not only improves satisfaction, but also optimizes the use of the company's resources, maximizing profitability and loyalty.

Chapter 7

Break the ice to strike up a conversation

- "Breaking the ice is the first step in building a relationship with the customer; It's about connecting with them on a personal level before addressing any sales topic."
  — *Tom Hopkins, "How to Master the Art of Selling"*

Breaking the ice in sales is an art that defines the course of all future customer interactions. It's the moment when the first impression is established, initial trust is built and the foundation for a fruitful conversation is laid. Achieving a quick and effective connection with the customer early on can be the difference between winning or losing a sale. This chapter delves into the techniques and skills needed to open a conversation naturally, generate an emotional connection, and overcome initial barriers.

7.1 The psychology of the first encounter

The human brain makes unconscious decisions about people in a matter of seconds. According to a study by **Princeton University**, people form a first impression in less than 10 seconds, which implies that the first moments of an interaction are crucial for any salesperson.

Key factors influencing first impressions:
1. **Physical appearance and personal presentation**: Dressing appropriately for the occasion and maintaining a neat appearance builds confidence.
2. **Body language**: An open and receptive body language, such as a relaxed posture and a warm smile, invites interaction.
3. **Tone of voice**: A friendly and confident tone creates a collaborative atmosphere.
4. **Empathy and sympathy**: Showing genuine interest and finding common ground helps disarm any potential resistance.

The goal in this first meeting is not to sell immediately, but to generate a sense of comfort and familiarity that allows the conversation to continue in a relaxed atmosphere.

Example:
Imagine a salesperson walking into a meeting room where a potential customer is already seated. The salesperson takes a few seconds to observe the surroundings and decides to start with a comment on a piece of art on the wall, which he notes appears to be a local piece. This generates a short, friendly conversation about the local culture before moving on to business, relaxing the customer and setting a friendly tone for the rest of the meeting.

7.2 Icebreaker techniques

Breaking the ice is not a mechanical process; It requires flexibility, observation, and quick adaptation to the client's signals. There are various techniques that can be applied depending on the context, the environment and the personality of the client.

7.2.1 Open-ended questions
Open-ended questions are those that can't be answered with a simple "yes" or "no," which stimulates a broader conversation and generates more interaction.

Examples of open-ended questions:
- "Tell me, how did you decide to expand into the market at this time?"
- "I'd love to hear more about how you guys handle [relevant issue] in your company."
- "What has been the most important thing to you in terms of [product/service]?"

Open-ended questions invite the customer to share more details, which not only helps break the ice, but also provides valuable insights into their needs and expectations.

7.2.2 Comments on the environment
Observing and commenting on details of the customer's environment is a subtle way to generate a conversation without seeming forced. It can be something as simple as a piece of décor, a family photo, or some detail of the environment that reveals something about the customer.

Tips for making appropriate feedback about the environment:
1. **Relevance**: The comment must be genuine and related to the immediate environment, such as a piece of art, a view from the window, or a visible acknowledgment.
2. **Subtlety**: Avoid overly personal comments that may make the customer uncomfortable.
3. **Moderation**: After the comment, it's important to give the customer space to continue the conversation.

Example:
A salesperson walking into a customer's office notices a photograph of a marathon on the wall. With a friendly smile, he comments: "It looks like you're a runner. Do you participate in a lot of marathons?" Not only does this feedback break the ice, but it can establish a personal connection with the customer, creating an atmosphere of camaraderie.

7.2.3 Finding common ground
People like to deal with those they feel a connection with. When the salesperson is able to find common ground with the customer, whether in terms of personal or professional interests, it is easier to build trust and break down initial barriers.

Techniques to find common ground:
- **Pre-research**: Before a meeting, the salesperson can do some research on the customer, their company, their role, and possible common interests.

- **Listen carefully**: While the customer is talking, pay attention to small details that may signal shared interests.
- **Share similar experiences**: Once a common ground is identified, it is helpful to share similar personal or professional experiences.

Example:

A salesman of financial solutions discovers, during the conversation, that the customer attends the same industry conferences that he has attended. Mentioning past experiences at these conferences helps to establish an immediate connection, generating a more relaxed and enjoyable atmosphere.

7.3 Overcoming initial barriers of resistance

Sometimes, customers can be reserved or reluctant at the start of a conversation. This initial resilience can be due to different factors, such as negative past experiences with sellers or simply disinterest in supply. Breaking the ice in these cases may require a more delicate approach.

7.3.1 Spot signs of resistance

Signs of resistance can be verbal or nonverbal:
- **Crossing your arms**: It can indicate a defensive posture.
- **Frequently looking at the clock or phone**: A sign of disinterest or impatience.
- **Short answers**: The customer avoids delving into the conversation, which may indicate a lack of interest or discomfort.

7.3.2 Strategies to reduce resistance

1. **Empathy**: Recognize the customer's emotional state. If the customer seems tense or busy, a good strategy is to say something like, "It sounds like this is a hectic time for you. If you prefer, we can schedule this meeting for another time."
2. **Validation**: Validate any concerns the customer may have. For example: "I know you may have had past experiences that weren't satisfactory. I'm here to listen to any questions you may have."
3. **Flexibility**: Offer the customer options or allow them to guide the conversation. Sometimes, giving the client control can reduce initial resistance.

Example:

A salesperson detects that the customer is restless and seems rushed during the meeting. Instead of continuing with a lengthy presentation, she decides to pause and ask, "I see you have a very tight schedule. Would you like us to focus on a couple of key points for now?" This strategy allows the client to relax, knowing that their time will be valued.

7.4 Digital communication

In today's world, many interactions with potential customers happen through digital means: emails, social media, or video calls. Although the format is different, icebreaker principles are still applicable, but with some adaptations.

7.4.1 Icebreaker in Emails

Emails are often the first point of contact with a customer, and the way the message is worded can make all the difference. An effective email should be personal, brief, and should show that the salesperson has done their homework on the customer.

Tips for effective emails:
- **Attractive subject line**: The subject line of the email should grab attention immediately, without being too pushy.
- **Personalization**: Avoid generic templates and refer to specific details of the customer or their company.
- **Clear value proposition**: Clearly state how the interaction will benefit the customer from the start.

Conclusion

Breaking the ice is a crucial component in the sales process, and mastering this skill can open doors that would otherwise remain closed. Through empathy, observation, and the use of open-ended questions or intelligent feedback, salespeople can overcome initial tension and establish a connection with the customer.

Chapter 8

Active listening

- "80% of sales success is due to the ability to listen and understand what customers really want."

— *Brian Tracy, "The Psychology of Selling"*

Active **listening** is a critical skill for any sales professional. Beyond simply listening to what the customer is saying, it involves paying attention, understanding, and responding appropriately to the customer's needs and concerns. This skill not only allows you to capture key information, but also helps build a relationship of trust, which is essential for successful sales. In this chapter, we'll explore active listening techniques, their benefits, and how to implement them in the sales process.

8.1 What is active listening?

Active listening refers to the ability to pay full attention to the interlocutor, not only to the words they use, but also to tone, emotions, and nonverbal cues. According to psychologist **Carl Rogers**, one of the leading theorists of active listening, this is one of the most effective forms of communication, as it promotes a deep and sincere understanding between the parties.

Components of active listening:
1. **Mindfulness**: It involves concentrating completely on what the client is saying, eliminating internal and external distractions.
2. **Emotional interpretation**: Capturing not only what the client says, but also how they say it, and what their emotions reveal.
3. **Validation**: Confirm that you have correctly understood the customer's message, which can be done by repeating or rephrasing what they have expressed.
4. **Constructive feedback**: Respond appropriately to advance the conversation and address the customer's concerns or questions.

Active listening helps the salesperson grasp details that can be crucial in identifying the customer's needs and offering a customized solution.

8.2 Benefits of active listening in sales

Active **listening** has a direct impact on sales effectiveness. Salespeople who master this skill often stand out for their ability to generate empathy and trust, two key factors for sales success. Let's look at some of the main benefits:

1. **Build trust**
   Customers trust salespeople more who listen carefully and show a genuine interest in understanding their needs. Not only does this increase the chance of closing a sale, but it also supports long-term relationships.

Example:
A customer expresses frustration with previous solutions that haven't worked. The actively listening salesperson responds, "I understand that you've had problems in the past. I'd like to focus on those aspects and find a solution that really works for you." This empathy-based approach builds a relationship of trust.

2. **Identify unexpressed needs**
   Many times, customers are not fully aware of what they need. Active listening helps identify those implicit needs, allowing the salesperson to offer a solution that the customer hadn't considered.

Example:
   A customer may mention that they are looking for a product that saves them time, but through active listening, the salesperson discovers that what they are really concerned about is the lack of staff to manage growth. By understanding this underlying need, the salesperson can suggest a more comprehensive solution.

3. **Makes it easier to overcome objections**
   Customer objections are often related to fears or concerns that may not be directly expressed. By practicing active listening, marketers can grasp the real reasons behind objections and address them effectively.

Example:
   If a customer expresses that the price is high, active listening can help discover that the real problem is not the price, but the perceived value of the product. The salesperson can then focus the conversation on highlighting the benefits and return on investment.

4. **Improves long-term relationship**
   Active listening is not only useful for closing a sale, but it also contributes to customer loyalty. Customers who feel heard and understood are more likely to return and recommend the salesperson to others.

Example:
   A salesperson who demonstrates a deep understanding of the customer's needs and offers customized solutions not only closes the current sale, but also creates a long-lasting relationship that leads to future sales.

8.3 Active listening techniques

Implementing active listening requires practice and the use of certain techniques that allow the salesperson to better grasp the information that the customer shares. Some of the most effective techniques are described below:

1. **Paraphrasing**
   Paraphrasing consists of repeating in your own words what the client has said, to confirm that you have understood correctly. This also shows the customer that you're paying attention.

Example:
Customer: "We've been struggling to handle the increase in demand, but we don't want to compromise on quality."
Salesperson: "It seems like growth has been challenging, and their main concern is maintaining quality while handling more volume. Is that so?"

2. **Emotional reflection**
   This technique involves recognizing and verbalizing the emotions that the client is conveying, which shows empathy and understanding.

Example:
Customer: "I'm really frustrated that the last three solutions we tried didn't work."
Salesperson: "I can tell you're frustrated with the solutions above. I understand how that can be discouraging."

3. **Strategic silence**
   Silence, well used, is a powerful tool for active listening. Allowing a quiet space after the customer speaks gives them a chance to reflect and share more information.

Example:
After the customer expresses a concern, the salesperson remains silent for a few seconds, often leading the customer to offer more details or clarifications.

4. **Nonverbal cues**
   Nonverbal cues, such as nodding your head, maintaining eye contact, and having an open posture, are crucial to show that you are actively paying attention.

8.4 Obstacles to active listening and how to overcome them

While active listening is critical to effective communication, it can also present challenges. Below, we discuss some of the most common obstacles and how to overcome them:

1. **External distractions**
   In an environment full of distractions, such as a noisy office or a phone conversation interrupted by notifications, it's easy to lose focus. To avoid this, it's essential to minimize distractions whenever possible. Turning off the phone, closing emails, or choosing a quiet environment for conversation are all effective actions.

2. **Selective listening**
   Selective listening occurs when the salesperson focuses only on the parts of the conversation that interest them, ignoring information that could be crucial. To overcome this, it is necessary to practice attentive listening and make a conscious effort to absorb all information, not just that which aligns with one's own interests.

3. **Disrupt the customer**
   Interrupting the customer or rushing the conversation can make it difficult to build trust and make the customer feel like they're not valued. It is essential to allow the client to finish speaking before formulating a response, and if necessary, clarification can be requested after the client has finished expressing their ideas.

4. **Prejudices and assumptions**
   It's easy to fall into the trap of making assumptions about what the customer needs before they've finished explaining their circumstances. To avoid this, sellers should keep an open mind and avoid jumping to conclusions before getting all the details.

Conclusion

Active listening is one of the most powerful tools a salesperson can master. Not only does it allow the seller to gain valuable information, but it also helps build strong relationships based on trust and mutual understanding. By using techniques such as paraphrasing, open-ended questions, and emotional recognition, salespeople can better connect with their customers and offer more personalized and effective solutions.

Chapter 9

Consultative selling and the power of Storytelling

- "Consultative selling is not about selling a product, but about solving a problem. And storytelling is a powerful tool to illustrate how this can be achieved."

    — *Michael Bosworth, "Solution Selling"*

Consultative **selling** is an approach that focuses on deeply understanding the customer's needs and problems, and then delivering customized solutions that generate value. Unlike traditional sales, which are primarily transaction-oriented, consultative selling focuses on building strong relationships and providing a solution that truly benefits the customer. One of the most powerful tools in this type of sale is **Storytelling**, or storytelling, which allows salespeople to connect emotionally with the customer, convey their message more effectively, and make the offer memorable. In this chapter, we will explore in depth how to implement consultative selling, the importance of storytelling in sales, and how to tell stories that reinforce the value proposition and foster trust.

9.1 What is consultative selling?

Consultative **selling** is an approach that prioritizes the role of the salesperson as an advisor or consultant, whose main objective is to help the customer solve their problems. This approach is based on relationship building and a deep understanding of the client's needs and goals. More than closing a quick sale, the purpose of consultative selling is to establish a long-term relationship based on trust and value contribution.

9.1.1 Key features of consultative selling

Consultative selling is distinguished from other types of sales by several key elements:

- **Customer focus**: The salesperson acts as an advisor, takes a genuine interest in the customer's challenges, and is committed to finding the most suitable solution.
- **Active listening**: The salesperson listens carefully, asks deep questions, and spends time understanding the customer's needs, concerns, and goals.
- **Customized value proposition**: The solution presented is tailored to the customer's specific circumstances, rather than following a pre-set script.
- **Long-term relationship**: The salesperson builds a relationship that goes beyond a single transaction, seeking to be a reliable partner in the customer's growth and success.

9.1.2 Benefits of consultative selling

Consultative selling not only improves the customer experience, but also offers important benefits for the salesperson and the company:

- **Increased customer loyalty**: By offering solutions that truly add value, the customer develops greater loyalty to the salesperson and the company.
- **Stronger closings**: Customers who perceive tangible value in the offer are more willing to compromise and close the sale.
- **Less price sensitivity**: When the customer understands the value that the solution brings, price becomes less important, as they perceive the cost as an investment.
- **Upsell opportunities**: A trusting relationship and deep understanding of the customer can open the door to future cross-selling and upselling opportunities.

9.2 Introduction to Storytelling in Sales

Storytelling is the ability to tell stories effectively to connect with the customer on an emotional and rational level. In sales, storytelling allows the salesperson to communicate their message in a way that captures attention, arouses interest, and generates an emotional connection. Well-told stories are remembered for much longer than facts and figures, and they have the power to change perceptions, influence decisions, and motivate action.

9.2.1 Why is Storytelling effective in sales?
Storytelling is effective in sales for several reasons:

- **Emotional connection**: Stories appeal to emotions, and purchasing decisions are often influenced more by emotional factors than rational ones.
- **Clarity and simplicity**: Stories can explain complex concepts in a simple and easy-to-understand way.
- **Memorability**: Customers remember stories much more easily than siloed data, making the offer more memorable.
- **Persuasion**: A good story can influence the customer's perceptions and beliefs, helping them to see the product or service in a more favorable light.

9.2.2 Elements of a Good Sales Story
For a story to be effective in sales, it must include several key elements:

1. **Protagonist**: Every story needs a main character with whom the customer can identify. This can be the customer themselves, another previous customer, or even the salesperson.
2. **Conflict or problem**: The story must pose a challenge or problem that the protagonist must solve. This conflict must be related to the customer's needs or problems.
3. **Solution**: Here the solution that the seller offers is introduced. It is important that the solution is not presented in a forced way, but that it is naturally integrated into the story.
4. **Result**: The story must conclude by showing the benefits of the solution and how it improved the protagonist's situation. This reinforces the value proposition of the product or service.

9.3 Storytelling strategies for consultative selling

Storytelling is a versatile tool that can be applied at various stages of the consultative selling process. Below, some specific strategies for integrating storytelling into the different phases of consultative selling are described.

9.3.1 Storytelling for Trust-Building

In the initial phase of consultative selling, the main goal is **to gain customer trust** . Here, stories about other customers who faced similar problems and found a satisfactory solution can be very effective.

- **Example**: "One of my clients, who had a company similar to yours, was facing major challenges in improving their operational efficiency. We tried several solutions, and finally, after implementing this strategy, they managed to reduce their costs by 20% in just six months."

9.3.2 Storytelling to identify needs

During the discovery phase, storytelling can help create a context in which the client feels comfortable sharing their needs and challenges. Telling a story about a relevant issue encourages the customer to open up and share their own experiences.

- **Example**: "I recently worked with a company that was experiencing difficulties similar to the ones you mentioned. Their main problem was the lack of visibility into their sales data. Has something similar happened to you?"

9.3.3 Storytelling to present the solution

In the solution presentation phase, storytelling can be used to illustrate how the product or service can solve the customer's problem in a concrete and visual way.

- **Example**: "A client of ours, who was also in the manufacturing sector, was able to improve the quality of their products and reduce production time by 30% thanks to our software. I imagine this would be very valuable to you as well, given the focus on efficiency that you have told me about."

9.3.4 Storytelling to overcome objections

Objections are natural in any sales process, and storytelling can be a powerful tool to address them effectively. By telling stories of other customers who had similar objections and overcame their doubts, you can help the customer feel more confident and confident.

- **Example**: "At first, another customer had similar concerns about cost. However, after analyzing the return on investment, he realized that the savings generated far exceeded the initial investment. In fact, the return was so positive that he ended up expanding the use of our solution to other areas of his business."

9.3.5 Storytelling to close the sale

In the final stage, when you're close to closing the sale, an inspiring story can help convince the customer to take the final step. The story should reinforce the idea that making the purchase decision will bring you significant benefits.

- **Example**: "I remember when a customer made the decision to implement our system in their company. At first, he was a little nervous, but he soon realized that it was the best decision. In the first year, he increased his productivity by 50%, and now he sees us as a key partner in his success. I would love it if we could achieve similar results for you."

9.4 Storytelling Case Studies in Consultative Selling

9.4.1 SMB Software Company

Context: A business management software vendor meets with a small manufacturing company that is looking to improve its operational efficiency.

- **History**: "A while ago, we worked with another company in the manufacturing sector that had very similar challenges. Their main problem was the time they were wasting due to the lack of integration between their systems. After implementing our software, they were able to reduce processing time by 40%, allowing them to deliver faster and improve customer satisfaction. Not only did they increase their efficiency, but they also achieved significant savings. Can you imagine the impact something similar could have on your operation?"

9.4.2 Human Resources Consulting

Context: An HR consultant meets with a company that is experiencing high turnover and wants to improve its retention strategy.

- **Story**: "I had a client a couple of years ago who was in the same situation. Its staff turnover was very high, and that was costing it a lot of money and resources. After conducting a deep analysis, we discovered that employees did not feel valued, and we created a recognition and professional development program. In less than a year, they managed to reduce turnover by 60% and the team's morale improved tremendously. I imagine something similar could be very beneficial for your company, don't you think?"

9.4.3 Fintech Company

Context: A vendor of financial software solutions meets with a small bank looking to improve its security system and reduce the risk of fraud.

- **History**: "We worked with a regional bank that was facing serious fraud problems, which was costing them large sums of money and damaging the trust of their customers. We implemented our security system and, in less than six months, they managed to reduce fraud attempts by 70%. In addition, their customers highly valued the improvement in security, which allowed them to increase their customer base. Do you think a solution like this could benefit your bank as well?"

9.5 Advanced Storytelling Techniques in Consultative Selling

9.5.1 The Hero's Journey Technique

The **Hero's Journey** is a classic narrative structure that can be very effective in sales. This technique presents the customer as the hero of the story, facing challenges and managing to overcome them thanks to the help of the salesperson and his solution.

- **Structure**: Introduction of the hero (client), presentation of the problem, meeting with the guide (salesperson), implementation of the solution, overcoming the challenge and final triumph.
-
- **Example**: "Just like you, our client was facing big challenges. But, together, we found a solution that not only solved the problem, but also took it to a whole new level of success."

9.5.2 The Technique of Transformation History

The **transformation story** focuses on how the solution radically changed a customer's situation. This approach highlights the "before" and "after" in a clear and visual way.

- **Structure**: Presentation of the initial state, implementation of the solution and description of the improved state.
-
- **Example**: "Before implementing our solution, the customer was losing customers and was unable to meet demand. Today, its operation is optimized and has doubled its capacity, which has allowed it to expand its business into new markets."

9.5.3 The Emotional Testimony Technique

Emotional **testimony** uses stories of customers who, in addition to achieving tangible results, experienced a positive change in their well-being or that of their team. This adds an emotional layer that reinforces the connection with the customer.

- **Structure**: Presentation of the client, description of the problem, how it affected emotionally, implementation of the solution, and positive emotional impact.
- **Example**: "Not only did our client improve their financial results, but they now feel calmer and more satisfied, knowing that they have a solution to back them up. She even mentioned that this has allowed her to sleep better and enjoy her personal life more.

Practical Concepts and Examples

Consultative **selling** has become a must-have approach for those looking to go beyond a transaction and develop long-lasting relationships with their customers. In this method, the salesperson acts as an advisor, focused on thoroughly understanding the customer's needs and challenges in order to offer customized solutions that add real value. Unlike traditional selling, consultative selling prioritizes relationship and long-term value over immediate closing.

This chapter explores in greater detail the key concepts of consultative selling and provides practical examples to illustrate how to apply this approach effectively in different sales situations.

9.6 Fundamental concepts of consultative selling

Consultative selling is characterized by its focus on the customer. The main pillars of this approach are described below:

9.6.1 Focus on the relationship

In consultative selling, the goal is **to develop a relationship of trust and collaboration** with the customer. This means that the salesperson is committed to understanding not only the customer's explicit needs, but also their long-term goals and the factors that could affect their success. To achieve this, the seller must:

- **Know the customer's context**: Understand the industry, the market, and the specific challenges the customer faces.

- **Be a strategic partner**: Position yourself as an ally willing to help the customer achieve their goals, rather than just selling a product or service.

9.6.2 Deep understanding of customer needs

A central element of consultative selling is the **ability to correctly diagnose** customer needs. To achieve this, the salesperson must employ **active listening** and ask strategic questions that uncover the customer's true challenges. This includes:

- **Ask open-ended questions**: Allow the client to express themselves broadly about their needs and expectations.
- **Identify explicit and implicit needs**: The former are those that the client recognizes and expresses clearly. Implicit ones are those that the customer may not mention but that are critical to their success.
- **Verify information**: Confirm with the client that their situation has been properly understood before submitting a proposal.

9.6.3 Solution Customization

Unlike other sales approaches, in consultative selling there is no one-size-fits-all solution. The seller must **customize the offer** to fit the customer's situation specifically, which involves:

- **Adapt the value proposition**: Present only the aspects of the solution that are relevant to the customer.
- **Use Storytelling**: Integrate stories from other customers who have experienced similar problems and how the solution helped them, making it easier for the customer to visualize the benefit of the solution.

9.6.4 Building a Long-Term Relationship

Consultative selling does not end with the closing of the sale. The aim is **to foster an ongoing relationship** that allows for future business opportunities and long-term loyalty. This involves:

- **Follow up**: Be available after the sale to answer questions, provide support, and make sure the customer is getting the most benefit.
- **Seek feedback**: Listen to the customer's experience with the solution to identify areas for improvement and possible new needs.
- **Be an ongoing resource**: Offer advice and recommendations on a regular basis, demonstrating that the customer is valued beyond the initial sale.

9.7 Step-by-step consultative selling process

Consultative selling can be divided into several stages, each with a specific goal and focus:

9.7.1 Preparation
Before the meeting with the customer, the salesperson must prepare thoroughly. This involves researching the client's business, their industry, their competitors, and market trends.

9.7.2 Building trust
During the first contact, the goal is **to establish trust and show genuine interest** in the customer. Active listening and empathy are essential at this stage.

9.7.3 Discovery of needs
Here, the salesperson asks strategic questions to identify the customer's needs and goals. It is essential to ask open-ended questions and listen carefully.

- **Example:** The salesperson asks, "What are the biggest challenges you are currently facing in your production process?" and "How would these challenges impact your operation if they are not solved in the short term?" These questions allow the salesperson to understand the context and discover areas where their solution could add value.

9.7.4 Introducing the custom solution
With a clear understanding of the customer's needs, the salesperson presents a solution **tailored** to the specific problems identified. Here, storytelling can be especially useful to illustrate how the product or service can make a difference.

- **Example:** "We have worked with several manufacturing companies that were facing similar productivity problems. We implemented a solution that allowed them to reduce their production times by 20% in the first year. I imagine this could be of great help to you as well."

9.7.5 Handling objections
In consultative selling, objections are an opportunity to deepen the relationship and better understand the customer. Instead of avoiding them, the salesperson should address them directly and with empathy.

9.7.6 Closing of the sale

In consultative selling, the closing should be natural and without pressure. The seller confirms that the customer is satisfied with the proposed solution and offers clear options to proceed.

Example: The salesperson summarizes how the solution responds to each of the needs discussed and asks the customer if they have any other concerns. Once the customer is comfortable agreeing to the solution, the salesperson presents the agreement and asks, "Is it okay for us to schedule delivery for Friday or Saturday?"

9.7.7 Ongoing monitoring and support

Consultative selling does not end at closing. The salesperson must follow up to ensure that the customer is satisfied and that the solution is meeting their expectations.

- **Example**: A few months after delivery, the salesperson schedules a follow-up meeting with the customer to review the results. He also stays available for any questions or additional support, showing that he cares about customer success.

9.8 Practical examples of consultative selling in various sectors

9.8.1 Consultative selling in information technology

Context: A company that specializes in cybersecurity solutions meets with a company that has experienced an increase in attempted cyberattacks.

- **Process**:
  - **Discovery**: The salesperson asks about the customer's concerns about the security of their data and the potential risks they face.
  - **Personalization**: After identifying that the customer's biggest challenge is phishing attacks, the salesperson adapts the proposal to focus on an advanced threat detection and response system.
  - **Storytelling**: The salesperson tells the story of a previous customer who implemented the same solution and managed to reduce attacks by 70% in six months.
  - **Follow-up**: After implementation, the vendor offers additional training to the customer's team and periodically reviews security reports to ensure that the system is operating optimally.

9.8.2 Consultative selling in financial consulting

Context: A financial consultant meets with a medium-sized company that is interested in optimizing its cost structure and increasing its profitability.

- **Process:**
    - **Discovery**: The consultant asks about the company's long-term financial goals and current challenges in terms of expenses and cash flow.
    - **Customization**: Based on the challenges identified, the consultant proposes an in-depth cost analysis and presents a cost reduction plan that aligns with the client's profitability goals.
    - **Storytelling**: The consultant shares a case where he helped another company reduce their costs by 25% in one year, which allowed them to invest in new areas of growth.
    - **Follow-up**: After the implementation of the plan, the consultant meets with the client every quarter to review the results and make adjustments as needed.

9.8.3 Consultative selling in the human resources sector

Context: An HR consultant meets with a company that has turnover issues and low levels of satisfaction in its team.

- **Process:**
    - **Discovery**: The consultant asks questions to understand the causes behind turnover and gathers information about current employee retention and satisfaction policies.
    - **Customization**: Based on the problems identified, the consultant proposes an improvement plan that includes a professional development program and a personalized incentive system.
    - **Storytelling**: The consultant tells the story of another company that implemented a similar program and managed to reduce its staff turnover by 30%, while employee engagement increased significantly.
    - **Follow-up**: The consultant provides follow-up through satisfaction surveys and regular meetings to adjust the program and ensure that retention and satisfaction goals are being achieved.

9.9 Advanced techniques to maximize the impact of consultative selling

9.9.1 Application of emotional intelligence

Emotional intelligence allows salespeople to perceive and manage customer emotions effectively, tailoring their approach to the customer's emotional state and creating a more satisfying sales experience.

9.9.2 Using Diagnostic Tools

Using diagnostic tools, such as questionnaires or gap analysis, helps to obtain a more complete view of the customer's needs, improving the accuracy of the customized solution.

9.9.3 Data integration and analytics

Use **data and analytics** to support proposals and make fact-based recommendations. This reinforces the credibility of the seller and allows the solution to be justified with concrete examples.

Conclusion

Consultative **selling** and **storytelling** are powerful tools for building strong, long-lasting relationships with customers. By applying storytelling at every stage of the consultative selling process, salespeople can connect with their customers in a deeper and more meaningful way. Stories allow customers to see beyond products and services, helping them visualize how the solution can improve their lives or businesses.

Chapter 10

The Deming Chain and its application in sales

- "Improving quality reduces costs in the long run, and this includes sales. The Deming Chain reminds us that continuous improvement is key."

  — *W. Edwards Deming, "Out of the Crisis"*

The **Deming Chain**, based on the principles of continuous improvement and quality control, is a powerful tool that has been used in various sectors, especially in the manufacturing industry. However, its applications are not limited to that field. In sales, Deming's principles can be used to optimize processes, improve customer relationships, and maximize the efficiency of the sales team. This chapter explores in depth Deming's **PDCA** (Plan, Do, Check, Act) cycle and its practical application in sales to develop a culture of continuous improvement that increases effectiveness and competitiveness.

10.1 The Deming Chain: Concept and fundamentals

The **Deming Chain** is founded on the philosophy that continuous improvement is key to the success and sustainability of any organization. W. Edwards Deming, who developed this concept, promoted the idea that companies must constantly improve their processes to better satisfy their customers, reduce costs, and increase the quality of their products and services.

10.1.1 PDCA cycle (Plan, Do, Check, Act)

The **PDCA cycle** is the core of the Deming Chain and consists of four phases that are applied in a cyclical manner to ensure continuous improvement:

1. **Plan (P):** Identify opportunities for improvement and set specific objectives. In sales, this phase involves analyzing performance data, identifying problem areas, and defining strategies to address them.
2. **Do (D):** Implement the planned strategies. Here, the sales team implements new tactics, products, or approaches to improve performance.
3. **Verify (C):** Evaluate the results obtained. This phase consists of measuring the impact of the strategies implemented and determining whether they have achieved the proposed objectives.
4. **Act (A):** Take corrective actions based on the results. If the strategies were successful, they are standardized to be integrated into the regular process. If not, they are readjusted and reintroduced into the PDCA cycle to keep improving.

10.1.2 Deming Chain benefits in sales

The application of the PDCA cycle in sales helps to:

- **Identify opportunities for improvement** in a systematic manner.
- **Reduce errors** and improve operational efficiency.
- **Increase customer satisfaction** through continuous improvement of processes and services.
- **Facilitate adaptability** to changes in the market, allowing the sales team to adjust their approach in an agile and proactive way.

10.2 Application of the PDCA cycle in the sales process

The PDCA cycle can be adapted to each stage of the sales process, from prospecting to closing and after-sales service. Below is a description of how the various phases of the PDCA cycle can be applied to these stages to create a more efficient and results-oriented approach to sales.

10.2.1 Plan: Identify opportunities for improvement in sales

In the **planning** phase, the sales team should conduct a thorough analysis of the current process, including sales results, customer behavior, and competition. This stage involves collecting data and setting specific, achievable goals.

Examples of activities in the planning phase:
- **Sales Data Analysis**: Review sales reports to identify patterns, trends, and areas for improvement.
- **Setting sales goals**: Setting clear goals for the team, such as increasing sales by 10% in a quarter or reducing average close time.
- **Identifying roadblocks**: Determining issues or barriers that hinder the sales process, such as long turnaround times or lack of team training.

10.2.2 Do: Implementation of improvement strategies

In the **making** phase, the planned strategies are put into practice. This could include implementing new sales tactics, using new technology tools, or training salespeople in specific skills.

Examples of activities in the do-it phase:
- **Sales team training**: Train salespeople in new communication techniques or in the use of CRM tools.
- **Application of new prospecting techniques**: Test innovative prospecting methods, such as the use of automated email marketing campaigns.
- **Development of new sales materials**: Create presentations, videos or catalogs that improve the communication of the benefits of the product to the customer.

10.2.3 Verify: Evaluation of Results

The **verification** phase consists of measuring the results obtained and comparing them with the objectives established in the planning phase. This helps determine if and to what extent the strategies implemented have been effective.

Examples of activities in the verification phase:
- **Key Performance Indicator (KPI) Analysis**: Evaluate metrics such as the number of new customers, conversion rate, average close time, and customer satisfaction.
- **Gathering feedback**: Getting feedback from the sales team and customers to identify potential improvements.

- **Comparison with targets**: Determine whether sales targets have been achieved and, if not, identify the factors that have prevented them from being met.

10.2.4 Act: Implementing Corrective Actions

In the **action** phase, strategies are adjusted according to the results obtained. If the tactics were successful, they are standardized and become part of the regular process. If they were not effective, they are modified and retested in the PDCA cycle.

Examples of activities in the action phase:
- **Adjusting sales strategies**: Modifying tactics that have not yielded expected results, such as changing the prospecting approach or closing methodology.
- **Process standardization**: Formalize methods that have been successful to integrate into daily operations.
- **Additional training**: Identify areas where the team needs more training and provide them with resources to improve.

10.3 Practical implementation of the Deming Chain in sales

For the Deming Chain to be effective in the sales environment, it is essential to adapt it to the specific needs of the team and the market. Here are some practical considerations for applying the PDCA cycle in sales.

10.3.1 Aligning Sales Goals with the PDCA Cycle

To effectively implement the PDCA cycle, sales goals must be aligned with continuous improvement objectives. This means that goals should be **specific, measurable, achievable, relevant,** and **time-based** (SMART).

Example: If the goal is to reduce lead response time from three days to one day, the PDCA cycle can be used to evaluate and improve processes that affect response time, such as automating welcome emails or delegating tasks.

10.3.2 Continuous Monitoring and Agile Adjustments

The success of the Deming Chain in sales depends on **constant monitoring** and the team's ability to make agile adjustments based on data and feedback. The PDCA cycle must be repeated continuously to adapt to changes in the market and customer needs.

Example: The sales team reviews performance data on a weekly basis, and if they notice a drop in the conversion rate, they initiate a new planning phase to identify possible causes and develop an immediate action plan.

10.3.3 Fostering a culture of continuous improvement in the sales team

For the PDCA cycle to be sustainable, it is essential to develop a **culture of continuous improvement** throughout the sales team. This means fostering collaboration, continuous learning, and shared responsibility for results.

Example: Organize team meetings every month to review results, share learnings, and discuss new ideas for improvement. In addition, recognize and reward team members who actively contribute to the optimization of sales processes.

10.4 Examples of PDCA Cycle Application in different sales scenarios

To illustrate how the PDCA cycle can be applied in sales, let's consider some specific scenarios in which this approach can be used.

10.4.1 Improving the prospecting process

Context: A sales team identifies that the prospecting process is not generating enough quality leads.

- **Plan:** The team analyzes prospecting data and sets a goal to increase the number of qualified leads by 20% in three months. You decide to test new sources of leads, such as LinkedIn and webinars.
- **Do:** They implement campaigns on LinkedIn and host a monthly webinar to attract new leads.
- **Verify:** At the end of each month, they review the data of the leads obtained and their quality.
- **Act:** They adjust the approach according to the results. If LinkedIn is more effective, more budget is allocated to this platform. If the webinar doesn't have the expected impact, the presentations are optimized and different topics are tested.

10.4.2 Reduction of closing time

Context: The average closing time is 45 days and the goal is to reduce it to 30 days.

- **Plan:** The team reviews the data to identify stages of the sales process where there are delays. The goal is to reduce the closing time by 33% in six months.
- **Do:** They implement a new automated follow-up system that sends reminders to customers at key points in the process.

- **Verify:** They analyze closing times on a monthly basis and measure the effectiveness of automatic reminders.
- **Take action:** They adjust automated messages based on customer feedback and continue to streamline the process.

10.5 Long-term benefits of the Deming Chain

Implementing the PDCA cycle in sales not only improves individual processes, but also creates a **sustainable competitive advantage**. By cultivating a culture of continuous improvement, sales companies can stay agile and adapt quickly to changes in the market and customer needs.

10.5.1 Customer satisfaction
Customers notice and appreciate continuous improvement. A sales team that uses the PDCA cycle to constantly optimize the customer experience tends to build relationships of trust and loyalty.

10.5.2 Operational Efficiency
The continuous application of the PDCA cycle enables sales teams to improve operational efficiency, reduce costs, and maximize productivity. This results in a more agile and profitable operation.

10.5.3 Talent Development
The PDCA cycle encourages continuous learning and development in team members. Salespeople who are actively involved in identifying problems and creating solutions gain new skills and feel more engaged.

Conclusion

The **Deming Chain** and its PDCA cycle provide a flexible and powerful structure for continuous improvement in sales. By applying these principles, sales teams can adapt nimbly to changes, streamline processes, and deliver a better customer experience. Creating a culture of continuous improvement is the key to staying competitive and successful in the dynamic world of sales.

Chapter 11

Pipeline and Marketing in the sales process

- "The pipeline is not just a list of prospects; it is a representation of the sales and marketing flow that allows a company to sustain its growth."
— David A. Aaker, "Strategic Market Management"

The **sales pipeline** is an essential model for understanding and optimizing the flow of opportunities throughout the sales process. Complemented by an effective marketing strategy, the pipeline allows sales and marketing teams to collaborate more seamlessly, creating a cohesive process that maximizes conversions and improves the customer experience. In this chapter, we'll explore how to structure, manage, and optimize your sales pipeline, as well as the marketing tactics that can be applied at each stage of the process to boost opportunities and increase ROI.

11.1 What is a sales pipeline?

The **sales pipeline** is a visual representation of the stages that sales opportunities go through from first contact to closing. It allows sales teams to organize and manage their opportunities more efficiently, assessing what stage they are at and what actions are necessary to move towards closure. An effective pipeline provides a clear view of the status of each opportunity and helps identify bottlenecks in the sales process.

11.1.1 Importance of the pipeline in the sales process

The pipeline not only organizes sales opportunities, it also:

- **Provides visibility**: Helps salespeople and managers understand the status of each opportunity, making it easier to make decisions and plan resources.
- **Facilitates revenue prediction**: By analyzing the pipeline, companies can forecast future revenue based on the value of opportunities at each stage.
- **Identify opportunities for improvement**: Pipeline data allows you to identify problem areas, such as stages where opportunities stall, to take corrective action.
- **Optimize time management**: By knowing the status of each opportunity, salespeople can prioritize their time and effort on those that are most likely to close.

11.1.2 Sales pipeline structure

A typical sales pipeline includes the following stages:

1. **Prospecting**: Identification of potential customers who may be interested in the product or service.
2. **Qualification**: Evaluation of the opportunity to determine if you meet the necessary criteria to continue in the process.
3. **Proposal presentation**: Interaction with the customer to present an offer or value proposition.
4. **Negotiation**: The process of discussing and adjusting terms to meet the needs of both parties.
5. **Closing**: Final decision by the client and signing of the contract.
6. **After-sales**: Post-sale follow-up to ensure satisfaction and encourage customer loyalty.

Each stage of the pipeline involves a series of specific actions and tactics to maximize the likelihood that the opportunity will advance to the next stage.

11.2 Marketing strategies for each stage of the pipeline

For the sales pipeline to be effective, it is essential to coordinate marketing activities with each stage of the process. By applying targeted marketing tactics, you can optimize the movement of opportunities throughout the pipeline and maximize conversions.

11.2.1 Marketing at the prospecting stage

Prospecting is the first stage of the pipeline and aims to identify and capture the interest of potential customers. In this phase, marketing focuses on attracting quality leads through techniques that generate visibility and attract the target audience.

- **Marketing strategies:**
    - **Content marketing**: Create and distribute valuable content that attracts potential customers, such as blog articles, educational videos, infographics, and ebooks.
    - **Paid advertising (PPC):** Using ads on social media, search engines, and content platforms to capture the attention of new customers.
    - **SEO optimization**: Ensuring that the company's content is optimized for search engines, so that potential customers can easily find the brand when they search for related solutions.
    - **Events and webinars**: Organize online or in-person events that provide value and allow prospects to learn more about the company and its solutions.

11.2.2 Marketing at the qualification stage

In the **qualification** stage, the goal is to determine if the leads obtained meet the criteria to become real sales opportunities. Marketing can support this phase by providing tools that help assess the lead's level of interest and suitability for the company's offering.

- **Marketing strategies:**
    - **Lead scoring**: Implement scoring systems based on the lead's behavior and their level of interaction with the brand. These systems assign values to each lead based on their profile and actions, such as opening emails or attending events.
    - **Segmented email marketing**: Use personalized email campaigns to collect more information about leads, and thus help better qualify each one.

- **Advanced forms**: Through forms on the website, collect key information that helps assess the lead's readiness to move forward in the sales process.

11.2.3 Marketing at the proposal submission stage

Once the lead has been qualified, the next step is to **present the proposal** or solution that best suits their needs. Here, marketing supports sales by providing materials and tools that effectively communicate the benefits of the product or service.

- **Marketing strategies:**
    - **Custom presentations**: Create sales presentations that can be customized to each customer's specific needs.
    - **Case studies and testimonials**: Show examples of how the product or service has helped other customers with similar problems, which increases credibility.
    - **Demo Tools**: Provide access to trial versions or live demos that allow the customer to experience the product before making a decision.

11.2.4 Marketing at the negotiation stage

Negotiation is a critical stage where clients consider specific details such as price, terms, and conditions. Marketing should support this process by offering materials that reinforce the value proposition and address potential objections.

- **Marketing strategies:**
    - **Product Comparisons**: Provide detailed comparisons with competitors to demonstrate the product's unique advantages.
    - **Benefits and ROI brochures**: Create documents that highlight the benefits of the product and the return on investment, helping the client visualize the value they will obtain.
    - **Guarantees and satisfaction tests**: Offer risk-free proof, return policies, or warranties that ease customer concerns and give them confidence to move forward.

11.2.5 Marketing in the closing stage

During the **closing**, the client makes the final decision and formalizes the agreement. Here, marketing should support the customer's decision, making sure they are convinced of the benefits of their choice.

- **Marketing strategies**:
    - **Closing incentives**: Offering discounts, bonuses, or welcome packages to motivate closure.
    - **Personalized thank you messages**: Send personalized thank you emails or messages that reaffirm the customer's decision and celebrate their commitment.
    - **Clear and easy-to-sign contracts**: Use digital platforms that simplify the signing process, reducing friction and facilitating the conclusion of the sales process.

11.2.6 Marketing in the after-sales stage

After-sales is key to strengthening the relationship with the customer and fostering their long-term loyalty. Marketing plays an essential role at this stage to ensure satisfaction and offer ongoing support.

- **Marketing strategies**:
    - **Loyalty programs**: Implement rewards and loyalty programs that incentivize the customer to continue choosing the brand.
    - **Satisfaction surveys**: Send surveys to measure customer satisfaction and get feedback on their experience.
    - **Educational content and support**: Provide additional guides, tutorials, and resources that help the customer get the most out of the product or service.

11.3 Key metrics to monitor the sales pipeline

Constant pipeline monitoring is essential for measuring performance and making informed decisions. Below are some of the key metrics that allow you to evaluate the effectiveness of your pipeline and adjust your strategy as needed.

11.3.1 Conversion rate by stage

The **conversion rate per stage** measures the percentage of opportunities that advance from one stage to the next. This allows you to identify where in the pipeline more leads are lost and adjust strategies to improve these conversions.

11.3.2 Average opportunity value

The **average opportunity value** is calculated by dividing the total value of all opportunities by the number of opportunities in the pipeline. This metric helps forecast future revenue and assess whether the opportunities in the pipeline are sufficient to meet sales goals.

11.3.3 Average closing time

Average **time to close** measures the time it takes for an opportunity to move from prospecting to closing. A shorter close time usually indicates an efficient sales process, while long times can signal problems in the pipeline.

11.3.4 Win/Loss rate

The **win/loss ratio** measures the percentage of opportunities that convert into effective sales versus those that are lost. This metric allows you to identify the overall effectiveness of the sales team and helps develop strategies to reduce missed opportunities.

11.4 Management technologies and tools pipeline and marketing

Effective pipeline management and marketing integration at every stage are complex processes that can benefit from technological tools. Below are some of the most useful tools for optimizing your sales pipeline and collaboration with marketing.

11.4.1 Customer relationship management (CRM) software

CRM is the fundamental tool for managing the sales pipeline. CRMs allow sales teams to store information about customers and opportunities, automate tasks, and track the pipeline in detail.
- **Examples of popular CRMs**: Salesforce, HubSpot, Zoho CRM, and Pipedrive.

11.4.2 Marketing automation

Marketing automation **platforms** allow marketing teams to create and manage custom campaigns for each stage of the pipeline. These tools make it easy to segment leads, send automated emails, and collect data about customer behavior.
- **Examples of marketing automation platforms**: Marketo, Pardot, Mailchimp, and ActiveCampaign.

11.4.3 Data analysis tools

Data **analytics** is essential for monitoring pipeline performance and optimizing sales and marketing strategies. Analytics tools allow you to identify trends, measure KPIs, and make data-driven decisions.
- **Examples of data analysis tools**: Google Analytics, Tableau, and Power BI.

11.5 Advanced pipeline strategies and integrated marketing

To maximize pipeline effectiveness, it's helpful to adopt advanced strategies that integrate sales and marketing seamlessly. Here are some of these strategies:

11.5.1 Account-Based marketing (ABM)
Account-based marketing (ABM) is a strategy in which the marketing team focuses on specific, high-value accounts, customizing all communications and tactics for these particular accounts. ABM allows you to create a highly personalized approach that increases the likelihood of conversion.

11.5.2 Automated lead nurturing
Automated **lead nurturing** uses automation to provide relevant content to each lead based on their stage in the pipeline. This ensures that leads receive the right information at the right time, improving conversions.

11.5.3 Implementing AI and machine learning
Artificial **intelligence (AI)** and **machine learning** make it possible to analyze large volumes of data and predict customer behavior. These technologies can be used to optimize the pipeline by forecasting results and recommending customized strategies.

Conclusion

The sales pipeline and integrated marketing are critical to creating a streamlined and effective sales process. Collaboration between sales and marketing allows you to maximize opportunities, improve conversions, and deliver a more consistent and satisfying customer experience. The implementation of advanced technologies and customized strategies reinforces the ability of companies to adapt to market needs and strengthen their competitive position.

Chapter 12

Cold calling and techniques to perform them successfully

- "Cold calling is one of the litmus tests for any salesperson. It's not just about making a sale; it's about opening a door."

— Art Sobczak, "Smart Calling"

Cold **calling** continues to be a powerful tool in the sales process, especially for prospecting and attracting new customers. Although they may seem intimidating, a well-executed cold call can open doors, generate quality leads, and build long-term business relationships. In this chapter, we'll explore strategies and techniques for conducting cold calling effectively, minimizing rejection and maximizing conversion opportunities. In addition, a detailed script for making cold calls step by step will be presented, optimizing each interaction to achieve better results.

12.1 What is a cold call?

A **cold call** is a phone call made to a potential customer with whom the salesperson has had no prior contact and who has not expressed active interest in the products or services offered. The goal of cold calling is to pique the prospect's interest, start a conversation, and, if possible, schedule a meeting or presentation to dig deeper into the product or service.

12.1.1 Objectives of cold calling
The main objectives of a cold call are:
- **Introduce the company and the product**: Publicize who you are, what you stand for, and what your value proposition is.
- **Generate interest**: Capture the prospect's attention and motivate them to consider the product or service as a potential solution.
- **Identify needs**: Quickly understand if and how the prospect can benefit from the offer.
- **Arrange a follow-up meeting or call**: Ideally, reach an agreement for a second contact where more details can be presented.

12.1.2 Common cold calling challenges
Cold calling presents several challenges that marketers must overcome to be effective:
- **Initial resistance**: The prospect may be skeptical or even defensive when receiving an unexpected call.
- **Lack of time**: Prospects are often busy, which can make it difficult for them to spend time listening to the salesperson.
- **Rejection**: Cold calling often faces high rejection rates, so the salesperson should be prepared to handle rejection positively.

12.2 Preparing for successful cold calls

Preparation is key to making cold calls effectively. This involves researching, planning, and developing a flexible script that allows the salesperson to tailor the conversation based on the prospect's response.

12.2.1 Preliminary investigation
Before you make the call, it's important to research the prospect and your company. This allows you to personalize the call and show that the salesperson has done their homework, which increases credibility.
- **Identify the prospect's profile**: Know the prospect's position in the company, their role, and their possible responsibilities.

- **Know the company**: Research the industry, common challenges, and recent achievements of the company to better understand its potential needs.
- **Set specific goals**: Define what you hope to achieve with the call. This could be setting up a meeting, getting information, or simply gauging the prospect's interest.

12.2.2 Developing a script

A **script for cold calling** provides a structure that helps the salesperson guide the conversation and stay in control. The script should include:
- **Greeting and introduction**: A clear and professional introduction.
- **Attractive opening**: A short statement that captures the prospect's interest from the start.
- **Value proposition**: Briefly explain how the product or service can benefit the prospect.
- **Connecting question**: A question that allows you to discover if the prospect faces any challenges that the product or service can solve.
- **Call to action**: An invitation to set up a follow-up meeting or call.

12.2.3 Practice and adjust

Rehearsing the script and adjusting it according to the results is essential. Practice allows the salesperson to feel more comfortable and natural when making the call, while feedback from the first few calls helps identify which parts of the script need improvement.
- **Simulations**: Perform simulations with colleagues to get feedback and adjust focus.
- **Adjustments based on prospect response**: Adjust the script based on common objections or questions that are raised during actual calls.

12.3 Strategies and techniques for successful cold calling

In addition to a good script, there are specific techniques that can help make cold calling more effective and salespeople feel more confident and prepared to face objections.

12.3.1 Capturing attention immediately

In the first few seconds, the goal is to grab the prospect's attention and show that the call is worth their time. This is accomplished with an **opening statement** that generates curiosity or relates directly to the prospect's interests.
- **Example**: "Hello, [Prospect's Name]. I've done some research on [prospect's company] and I see that they've been growing rapidly.

Congratulations on that achievement. I'd like to share something that could help them expand that growth even further."

12.3.2 Adapting body language and tone of voice

Even in a phone call, **body language** can influence the prospect's perception. Maintaining an upright posture and a smile while speaking can be reflected in the tone of voice, projecting energy and confidence.

- **Tip**: Smile as you speak. This is noticeable in the tone and makes the salesperson seem more approachable and enthusiastic.

12.3.3 Asking open-ended questions

Open-ended **questions** allow the prospect to express themselves freely and provide valuable information. These types of questions help uncover specific needs and concerns that the salesperson can address.

- **Example**: "What main challenges does your team face in terms of efficiency in internal processes?"

12.3.4 Handling objections

Handling **objections** is a crucial part of cold calling. Instead of evading objections, the salesperson should respond to them with empathy and confidence.

- **Appreciation and response technique**: Thank the prospect for sharing their objection, validate their concern, and offer an answer that addresses the problem.
    - **Example**: "Thank you for mentioning it. I understand your concern about the budget. Many of our clients thought the same before seeing the return on investment this brought them. Would you like to see some examples of how others achieved positive results?"

12.3.5 Close the call with a clear call to action

At the end of the call, the salesperson should make it clear what the next step is. Whether it's setting up a meeting or sending additional information, the **call to action** should be straightforward and easy to understand.

- **Example**: "Is it okay if we scheduled a call next week to show you more in depth how we could help your team?"

12.4 Example of a script for cold calling

Below is a detailed script for a cold call, designed to guide the salesperson through every step of the conversation. This script is flexible and can be adapted to different industries and types of prospects.

Cold call script: Step by Step

1. Pre-preparation: Before you make the call, make sure you have the following information:
- Prospect Name and Title
- Basic information about the prospect's company
- Specific Call Objective

2. Greeting and introduction:
- "Hello, [Prospect's Name]. My name is [Your Name], and I call you from [Your Company Name]. Do you have a moment to talk?"

(Make sure the lead is available before proceeding.)

3. Opening statement to attract interest:
- "I was doing some research on [prospect's company] and saw that they specialize in [mentioning something relevant]. Congratulations on your growth in [specific area]. Precisely, we have worked with companies like yours to improve [area of interest]."

4. Presentation of the value proposition:
- "At [Your Company Name], we help companies optimize [area of interest] using [product or service]. In fact, we've been able to get our clients to improve their [relevant metrics, such as efficiency or profitability] by a [percentage]."

5. Connecting question:
- "Could you tell me a little bit about the current challenges your team is facing in relation to [area of interest]?"

(Listen carefully and take notes. This will help you tailor your approach based on the answer.)

6. Handling objections:
- Prospect: "We're not interested right now."
- Answer: "I completely understand. Often, our customers had similar doubts before they saw how we could add value to them. Could you briefly share with me what you consider to be the most important thing for your company right now?"

(This allows you to open up the conversation to other prospect needs and explore whether there's a way to tailor the proposal.)

7. Closing and call to action:
- "I would love to show you in more detail how we have helped others in your sector. How about scheduling a 15-minute meeting next week? That way, I can present you with more concrete examples and see if it really makes sense for your team."

8. Thank you and confirm the next step:
- "Thank you for your time, [Prospect's Name]. I will send you a confirmation email with the invitation to the meeting. Is that okay with you?"

(Be sure to send the confirmation immediately after the call and include relevant details.)

Conclusion

Cold calling is still a critical component of the sales process, especially when used strategically. The key to success lies in preparation, in the ability to adapt to the prospect's response and in a well-structured script that allows you to guide the conversation. By employing techniques such as active listening, handling objections, and a clear call to action, salespeople can significantly improve the effectiveness of their cold calling, making it a powerful tool for generating opportunities and building lasting relationships with new customers.

12.5 Example of Using Text Messages via WhatsApp to Close Sales

Social networks and messaging applications, such as **WhatsApp**, have become essential tools for communication with customers. They are especially useful in sales due to their immediacy, ease of use, and popularity. In this chapter, we'll explore how to structure effective messages on WhatsApp to capture the customer's attention, keep the conversation focused, and close the sale quickly and effectively. At the end, a **case study will be presented** with examples of step-by-step messages, from the initial greeting to the successful closing.

12.5.1 Advantages of using WhatsApp in sales
The use of WhatsApp in sales offers numerous advantages:
- **Immediacy:** WhatsApp allows almost instant communication, ideal for quick interactions and responding to queries in real time.

- **High level of personalization**: The possibility of using personalized texts, images, videos and files allows the message to be adapted to the customer's needs.
- **Higher open rate**: WhatsApp messages are usually opened and read more frequently than emails, increasing the likelihood of a response.
- **Ease of use**: Most people use WhatsApp, making it a familiar and accessible platform for customers of different profiles.

12.5.2 Strategies to write effective whatsapp messages for sales

To use WhatsApp effectively in sales, it's essential to structure messages in a short and direct way, ensuring that each interaction moves towards closing the sale.

1. Create an engaging opening greeting

The first message is crucial, as it sets the tone of the conversation and should grab the customer's attention quickly. An effective greeting on WhatsApp should be **personalized, short,** and should demonstrate **empathy** or **recognition** from the customer.

- **Example of an initial greeting**:
    - "Hi, [Customer's Name]! I am [Your Name] from [Company Name]. I saw that you were interested in [product/service]. Do you have a few minutes to talk about how it can help you?"

2. Keep the conversation short and to the point

Messages on WhatsApp should be concise and address the customer's needs directly. Each message must have a clear purpose, whether it is to answer a question, clarify a doubt or move towards closure.

- **Example of a concise message**:
    - "I understand, [Customer's Name]. With [product/service], you could save time and improve [specific benefit]. Would you like to know how it works in detail?"

3. Respond effectively to objections or questions

Objections are common in sales, and on WhatsApp it is important to respond quickly and with short answers. Effective responses should validate the customer's concern and offer an additional solution or advantage.

- **Example of an answer to an objection**:
    - Customer: "Isn't the product a bit expensive?"
    - Answer: "I understand your concern, [Name]. Many customers thought the same way before using it, but they achieved a return on investment that exceeded the cost in a

short time. Would you like to see some examples of how it has helped others?"

4. Create a direct call to action
Every message should include a **call-to-action** (CTA) that guides the customer to the next step. The CTA should be short and to the point, and it can include a question that motivates the customer to respond immediately.

- **Example call to action:**
    - "Is it okay if I send you a link to place the order? So you have it in minutes and with fast delivery."

12.6 Case study: Step by step in creating messages to close a sale on WhatsApp

Below is a case study detailing the step-by-step of how to structure messages to close a sale using WhatsApp.

1. First greeting and introduction message
- **Message:**
    - "Hi, [Customer's Name]! I am [Your Name] from [Company Name]. I saw that you have shown interest in [product/service]. Is it a good time for me to tell you a little more about how I could help you?"

2. Brief presentation of the value proposition
Once the customer responds, proceed with a brief description of the product or service, focusing on the value it will bring.

- **Message:**
    - "Great, [Customer's Name]. Our [product/service] has helped many people to [specific benefit, such as 'save time', 'improve productivity', or 'increase sales']. It is designed for [relevant feature], which allows for fast results. Is there anything specific you'd like to know about how it can benefit you?"

3. Respond to questions or objections
It is common for the customer to have questions or doubts about the product. Respond to each objection with empathy and provide a solution.

- **Example of objection:**
    - Customer: "Is it safe to use the system? It seems complex."
    - **Answer:** "Totally understandable, [Name]. In fact, the system has been designed to be easy to use and 100% secure. We

have advanced security protocols in place to protect your information. In addition, we offer support at all times to make you feel comfortable. Would you like to try it?"

4. Provide proof or demonstration (if appropriate)
If the customer is hesitant, offer a quick demo or trial so they can see the value of the product for themselves.

- **Message**:
  - "I understand that you prefer to try it before deciding. Would you like me to send you a link to explore a free demo? So you can see how it works and decide if it's for you."

5. Close the sale with a direct call to action
In the end, look to close with a CTA that invites the customer to make the purchase or schedule a follow-up, if necessary.

- **Closing message**:
  - "I'm glad to hear you're interested. I can send you the link to place the order right now and you can start using it as soon as you want. Would you like to proceed with the order?"

(If the customer still needs more time, offer a clear next step, such as scheduling a call or a more detailed demo.)

- **Alternative example**: "I understand that you want to think about it. Is it okay if I contact you tomorrow to find out if you have any questions or need more information?"

6. Thank you and order confirmation or follow-up
Be sure to close the conversation with a thank you message and confirm next steps, showing your availability for any additional queries.

- **Closing and thank you message**:
  - "Perfect, [Customer's Name]. Thank you very much for your interest. I'll send you the link shortly. I'm here for any questions you may have. Have a great day!"

(If a follow-up has been agreed, confirm the day and time and show willingness to resolve any questions in the future.)

Conclusion

WhatsApp and other messaging platforms are very powerful tools in the modern sales world. By mastering the art of structuring clear, direct, and personalized messages, salespeople can not only capture their customers' interest, but also close sales quickly and efficiently. This approach to direct and personalized communication, if handled properly, has the potential to build relationships of trust and generate effective conversions, making the most of the immediacy and accessibility offered by these platforms.

Chapter 13

Identify and counter objections in the sales process

- "An objection is simply a sign of interest. The salesperson's job is to address those objections in a way that makes the customer feel heard and understood."

  — *Zig Ziglar, "Secrets of Closing the Sale"*

Identifying and counterarguing objections is a critical skill for any sales professional. Objections are a natural part of the sales process, as customers often express doubts, concerns, or reservations before making a purchase decision. Learning how to handle these objections effectively not only helps reduce rejection, but also allows you to establish a relationship of trust and demonstrate the relevance of the solution offered. In this chapter, we'll explore how to identify different types of objections, best practices for responding to them, and advanced techniques for transforming objections into closing opportunities.

13.1 Understanding sales objections

Objections can arise at any point in the sales process, and they often reflect the customer's need for more information or clarification before feeling confident in making a decision. Understanding objections is the first step to handling them effectively.

13.1.1 What is an objection?
An **objection** is any concern, doubt, or reservation that the customer expresses during the sales process. Objections can be explicit, such as when the client expresses a concern openly, or implicit, when the client gives indirect signs of doubt.

13.1.2 Common types of objections
Objections can be classified into several categories, and each requires a different approach to address:

1. **Price objections**: The client feels that the cost is too high or not within their budget.
2. **Objections of necessity**: The customer is not convinced that he really needs the product or service.
3. **Urgency objections**: The customer does not feel that the purchase decision is urgent and prefers to postpone it.
4. **Objections of trust**: The customer has doubts about the company, the product or the seller, and does not feel confident about making the purchase.
5. **Time objections**: The customer claims not to have enough time to analyze the offer or make a decision at that time.

13.1.3 The importance of identifying objections
Identifying objections allows the seller to tailor their approach and provide the right information. In addition, by anticipating and preparing responses to common objections, the salesperson can prevent them from becoming insurmountable obstacles.

13.2 Techniques for identifying objections

It's not always apparent when a customer has an objection. Signals can be subtle, and that's why it's essential for the salesperson to be on the lookout for verbal and nonverbal cues that suggest a concern. Here are some techniques to identify objections more accurately:

13.2.1 Active listening

Active **listening** involves paying attention to what the customer says and how they say it. By doing this, the salesperson can pick up on the doubts that the customer is expressing, even if they don't do it directly.

- **Example:**
    - Customer: "The product looks interesting, but I'm not sure it will work for our type of company."
    - In this case, the doubt suggests that the customer might have an objection related to the product's suitability for their specific situation.
- **Active listening tip:** Paraphrasing and confirming what the customer is saying helps clarify your message and confirm if there is an implicit objection.
    - Salesperson: "So, you're telling me you're worried about whether the product is tailored to your company's specific needs? Could you tell me more about those requirements?"

Active listening is based on picking up on subtle signals and, at the same time, making the customer feel heard, which facilitates communication and builds trust.

13.2.2 Asking clarifying questions

When the client shows signs of a potential objection, it's helpful to ask questions that allow them to express their concern in more detail. This helps clarify the problem and determine how to respond appropriately.

- **Examples of clarifying questions:**
    - "Could you explain a little more about that?"
    - "What specifically concerns you about this aspect of the product?"
    - "What characteristics do you consider most important to you?"

Not only do these questions help identify objections, but they also show the customer that the salesperson is genuinely interested in understanding their needs, which can ease their concerns.

- **Case study:**
    - Customer: "I'm not sure if the price is fair for what you offer."
    - Salesperson: "I understand. Could you tell me what aspects of the price seem high to you relative to the benefits we have discussed?"

13.2.3 Reading body language

Body **language** can provide clues to the client's objections. If the customer seems uncomfortable, avoids eye contact, or crosses their arms, they could be hesitating or feeling insecure.

- **Signs of objection in body language:**
    - **Crossing their arms**: This can indicate that the client is feeling defensive or disagrees.
    - **Avoid eye contact**: It can suggest insecurity or lack of interest.
    - **Leaning back**: Indicates that the customer may be withdrawing from the conversation, which may be a sign of disinterest or doubt.
    - **Rubbing your hands or touching your face**: These are often signs of anxiety or self-doubt.

By spotting these signs, the salesperson can step in and ask questions to bring to light any objections the customer may have. For example, if a customer crosses their arms and seems uncomfortable, the salesperson might say:

- **Example:**
    - Salesman: "I see you're thoughtful. Is there anything that doesn't quite convince you?"

With this simple observation, the salesperson allows the customer to express their doubts, making them feel more comfortable and opening the door to an honest conversation.

13.2.4 Anticipation of objections

Based on experience and product knowledge, salespeople can anticipate common objections and address them before the customer expresses them, thus demonstrating proactivity and understanding of the customer's concerns.

- **Anticipation technique**: Incorporate phrases such as "Some of our customers were also wondering..." or "A common concern I've heard is..." It allows the salesperson to approach the issue in a preventive way and in a way that the customer can relate to their own doubts.
- **Example:**
    - Salesperson: "I know the price may seem steep at first. Many of our clients felt the same way until they understood the return on investment. Would you like to know more about how the value of our product outweighs the initial cost?"

Anticipating objections also allows the salesperson to prepare with solid responses tailored to potential rejections, improving their ability to counterargue quickly and effectively.

13.3 Techniques for countering sales objections

Once the objection has been identified, the next step is to handle it effectively. There are several techniques to address objections and turn them into opportunities to strengthen the relationship and move toward closing the sale.

13.3.1 Appraisal and response technique
This technique is based on **validating the customer's concern** and then responding in a way that demonstrates understanding and offers a different solution or perspective.

Steps to apply the appreciation and response technique:
1. **Validate the objection**: Start by acknowledging that the customer's objection is valid and understandable. This shows that you listened and understood their concern.
2. **Offer an informational response**: After validating, offer an answer that addresses the objection and provides information that demonstrates how the concern can be resolved.
3. **Reinforce the value proposition**: Conclude by highlighting how the product or service is still beneficial to the customer despite the objection.

Example:
- Customer: "The cost seems too high for our budget."
- Salesperson: "I completely understand. The initial investment may seem high, and it's a common concern. However, many of our customers found that the long-term savings quickly offset the initial cost, as they achieved [specific benefit, such as 'reduce operating costs' or 'improve efficiency']. I'd love to show you how some of them achieved a return on investment in the first six months."

This technique works well because it prevents the customer from feeling like their concern has been ignored or minimized, and it offers a clear path for them to see how the product can solve their concerns.

13.3.2 Reflex question technique
The **reflex question** returns the objection to the client so that they are motivated to reflect on their own concern. This technique helps to discover if the objection is genuine or if it hides a deeper doubt.

Steps to apply the reflex question technique:
1. **Listen to the customer's objection**: Make sure you fully understand what the customer is saying.
2. **Return the question**: Rephrase the objection in the form of a question to invite the client to reflect.
3. **Dig deeper into the Response**: Based on the customer's response, further explore the objection to understand the core of the problem and address it specifically.

Example:
- Customer: "I'm not sure it's the right time to make this purchase."
- Salesperson: "I get it. What factors do you think would indicate that this is the right time to invest in this solution?"

In this example, the salesperson invites the customer to analyze their own perception of proper time, which may lead to the discovery that the concerns may not actually be so much related to time, but to other aspects.

13.3.3 Social evidence technique
Showing how other people or companies have been successful using the product or service can help decrease customer hesitation. This technique is useful for trusting and urgency objections.

Steps to apply the social evidence technique:
1. **Present similar cases**: Describe other customers with similar characteristics or concerns and how their decision to purchase the product benefited them.
2. **Share concrete results**: Provide specific data or figures that demonstrate the success of other customers.
3. **Invite comparison**: Suggest that the client see themselves reflected in the case presented so that they can visualize how they could obtain similar results.

Example:
- Customer: "I'm not sure if this product will work for my company."
- Salesperson: "It's natural to feel that doubt. One of our customers in a similar situation implemented this product last year, and in just six months, they managed to increase their efficiency by 30%. I would love to share more details about your experience. Would you like to know how they did it?"

With this technique, the salesperson demonstrates that other people faced the same concerns and managed to overcome them with positive results, which inspires confidence in the customer.

13.3.4 Breakdown technique

Bid **breakdown** can help alleviate price objections by showing cost and value in more specific terms. This technique focuses on highlighting what the customer gets in exchange for price.

Steps to apply the breakdown technique:
1. **Break down price or offer**: Break down price into its components, such as additional features, benefits, or services.
2. **Explain the value of each component**: Detail how each part contributes to the total value and how the price is justified in terms of benefits.
3. **Compare with alternatives or hidden costs**: Shows how other alternatives may not include certain elements or may entail additional costs in the long run.

Example:
- Customer: "The price is higher than I expected."
- Salesperson: "Let me break down what's included in the total cost. You're not only getting the product, but also personalized training, 24/7 technical support, and ongoing updates. In addition, the system is designed to save [percentage of time or money] in your daily operations. Do you think these benefits justify the price in the long run?"

By applying this technique, the salesperson shows in detail the value the customer is getting, which helps mitigate cost-related objection and demonstrates the long-term return on investment.

13.3.5 "Yes, but..." technique

This technique uses a positive affirmation to acknowledge the objection and then presents a counterargument that reinforces the value proposition.

Steps to apply the "Yes, but..." technique:
1. **Accept the objection**: Acknowledge the objection without contradicting the client, using the "Yes".
2. **Redirect with a benefit**: Use the "but" to highlight a benefit that addresses the objection.
3. **Reinforce the advantage**: Expand on the answer by highlighting how the benefit is particularly relevant to the customer.

Example:
- Customer: "It seems like a huge investment of time to learn how to use this new system."
- Salesperson: "**Yes**, I can understand that initial training takes some time, **but** our customers have found that, once they become familiar with the system, they save a significant amount of time in their processes. Would you like to know more about what our training is like and how long it takes on average to get familiar with the system?"

This technique is useful for balancing acceptance of the client's concern with introducing a benefit that could change their perspective on the objection.

13.4 Practical examples of counter-argumentation of objections in sales

Below are examples of common objections and how to counter them using the techniques described.

Example 1: Price objection
- **Client Objection:** "This seems to be out of our budget."
- **Answer:** "I understand. Some of our customers had similar concerns until they saw the impact on their operating costs. If you consider long-term savings, you'll see that it really is an investment. Could we review together how this cost pays for itself over the course of the year?"

Example 2: Objection of necessity
- **Customer objection:** "I'm not sure if we really need this product."
- **Answer:** "I understand. Many of our customers didn't realize they needed it until they started to see it improve their operations. Have you considered how this product could solve [specific problem]? It could make a big difference."

Example 3: Objection of confidence
- **Client objection:** "I'm not sure you guys are the best fit for us."
- **Answer:** "I understand your concern, [Name]. We also believe that trust is key. We pride ourselves on our satisfied customers, such as [similar customer name], who have trusted us for years. If that's okay with you, we could set up a meeting to review any questions in detail and show you references from current clients."

Example 4: Urgent objection
- **Client objection:** "I don't think we have to decide this right now."

- **Answer**: "Totally understandable. However, some of our clients in similar situations found that delaying the decision meant missing out on certain opportunities for growth. Would you like me to show you some examples of how early implementation can benefit you?"

Example 5: Time Objection
- **Client's Objection**: "I don't have time for this right now."
- **Answer**: "I get it, I know he's busy. The good news is that our solution is designed to be easy to implement and requires very little time on your part. Would you be okay with scheduling a quick demo for next week?"

13.5 Advanced strategies for converting objections in sales opportunities

Learning to see objections as opportunities is essential for a successful salesperson. These advanced strategies allow you to turn objections into talking points that reinforce the value proposition.

13.5.1 Positive reframing of objections

Positive **reframing** involves changing the client's perspective on the objection, showing them how their concern can actually be an advantage.
- **Example**: If the customer says that the product is expensive, the salesperson might reply: "That is precisely the added value of our product: its high quality ensures a durability that others cannot offer."

13.5.2 Using Storytelling to address objections

Telling a story about a client who faced a similar situation can be a powerful way to overcome objections. This allows the customer to visualize the benefit of the solution in a context similar to their own.

- **Example**: "We had a customer in the same situation. At first, he was hesitant because of the cost, but after seeing the return on investment, he said it was one of the best decisions he ever made. I would love for him to be able to have the same experience."

13.5.3 Strengthening credibility with data and evidence

When the customer has doubts about the effectiveness of the product, the use of **concrete data and evidence** can help strengthen credibility.

- **Example**: "To make you feel more confident, I might share with you some case studies and data that show how our clients have improved in [specific outcome]. Would you like me to send them to you?"

13.6 Case Study

Script for handling objections in sales

Scenario: A potential client shows interest in a project management software, but has doubts about the cost and the real need for the investment.

Step-by-step script:
1. Presentation and value proposition
- Salesperson: "Hello, [Customer's Name]. I see that your team is looking to improve efficiency in project management. Our software has been proven to increase productivity by 25% in similar companies. What do you think?"

2. Price objection
- Customer: "Sounds good, but the cost is a bit high for us."
- Salesperson: "I understand, [name]. It's common for cost to be an initial concern. However, our customers found that the savings in man-hours and the improvement in the organization quickly justified the investment. Would you like to see some examples of ROI?"

3. Objection of necessity
- Customer: "I'm not sure if we need this advanced functionality."
- Salesperson: "Good observation. At first, many customers didn't realize how much they relied on advanced features until they saw the results. Are there any specific tasks that your team feels they could improve on?"

4. Closing and Call to Action
- Salesperson: "I understand your concerns, and I'm glad you shared them. If that's okay with you, we might offer you a free demo to try out the system and see how it can fit your needs. Would you like to schedule it this week?"

(The salesperson ends the conversation by offering a clear and accessible next step that allows the customer to experience the product without risk.)

Conclusion

Objections are opportunities in disguise, and knowing how to turn them into moments of learning and reflection is an essential sales skill. Strategies such as positive reframing, storytelling, using data and evidence, turning objections into discovery questions, and presenting viable alternatives allow the salesperson to transform doubts into bridges to closure. Handling objections effectively is an essential skill that can make the difference between losing a sale and gaining a loyal customer. By identifying, understanding, and countering objections, salespeople can transform potential roadblocks into opportunities to strengthen their value proposition. The key is to actively listen, respond with empathy, and offer solutions that highlight the benefits of the product or service in a clear and compelling way. With practice and the right techniques, objection handling becomes a powerful tool for closing sales effectively and building lasting relationships with customers.

Chapter 14

Sales Closing Strategies and Techniques to ensure customer engagement

- "The closing is the moment when all the sales effort materializes. It is the result of effective communication, empathy and understanding of the customer."

    — *Grant Cardone, "The Closer's Survival Guide"*

The closing of a sale is the culminating moment of the entire commercial process. It is the phase in which the seller and the customer consolidate an agreement that not only involves the final transaction, but also the beginning of a long-term value relationship. Achieving an effective closing requires specific skills and the mastery of several techniques that allow the salesperson to guide the customer to a satisfactory decision. In this chapter, we'll explore various advanced strategies and techniques for closing sales, as well as the psychology behind a successful closing. In addition, practical examples will be provided for implementing each closure technique effectively.

14.1 The importance of closing in the sales process

The **closing of sales** is the end point of the commercial interaction, but it is also the beginning of the customer relationship. A successful closing ensures that the customer is satisfied with their decision, which can lead to future sales opportunities, referrals, and a long-lasting relationship. In addition, it is crucial for the seller to meet their objectives and goals.

14.1.1 Closing objectives
The main objective of closing sales is to make the sale, but it also involves:
- **Confirm the client's commitment**: Make sure that the client is convinced of their decision and feels confident with the choice.
- **Create a positive experience**: Facilitate a frictionless transition from interest to purchase of the product or service.
- **Foster a long-term relationship**: Establish a solid foundation that allows for future sales, loyalty, and referrals.

14.1.2 Closing indicators
Recognizing the signs of closure is essential to knowing when the time is right to move towards the completion of the sale. Some indicators include:
- **Questions about specific details**: When the customer starts asking about delivery policies, payment terms, or warranties, it can be a sign that they're ready to close.
- **Verbal or nonverbal confirmation**: Statements such as "I find this helpful" or positive body language can indicate that the client is predisposed to closure.
- **Expression of urgency**: If the customer shows concern about making sure they get the product on time or avoid losing the offer, they may be ready to close.

14.2 Sales closing strategies: Main techniques

Below are several sales closing techniques that help ensure customer engagement. Each technique adapts to different scenarios and customer profiles, so it is important that the salesperson masters them and selects the most appropriate one according to the situation.

14.2.1 Closure by direct assumption
The **direct assumption** technique consists of acting as if the customer has already made the purchase decision, guiding them directly towards closing.

This technique is based on the premise that the customer is already convinced, and the salesperson simply assumes their commitment.

Steps to apply the closure by direct assumption:
1. **Assume customer engagement**: Use language that presupposes the customer's decision, such as "Let's proceed with..." or "So that you enjoy the product as soon as possible, we will make..."
2. **Detail next steps**: Explain to the customer what happens next, such as signing the contract, payment, or delivery.
3. **Request final confirmation**: Ensure that the client agrees to proceed, providing the opportunity to express any lingering doubts.

Example:
- Salesperson: "Perfect, then we're going to schedule delivery for next week. I just need a signature on the contract and we're good to go. Is that okay with you?"

This technique is particularly effective when the customer has shown clear signs of interest and has already expressed that the product is attractive or useful to them.

14.2.2 Closure of the alternative

Closing **the alternative** is useful for customers who show indecision. Instead of asking directly if they want to make the purchase, the salesperson presents two options, so that the customer does not decide whether or not to buy, but **how** they will do it.

Steps to apply the closure of the alternative:
1. **Offer two concrete options**: Present the client with two alternatives, both focused on moving towards closing.
2. **Highlight the benefits of both options**: Explain how each option meets the customer's needs.
3. **Allow the client to be in control**: This technique gives the client a sense of control as they make the final decision between two options.

Example:
- Seller: "We can proceed with the standard version and start rolling out next week, or, if you prefer, you can opt for the premium version, which includes additional support. Which one do you prefer?"

Closing the alternative is effective because it reduces the pressure on the customer by offering them options and, at the same time, directs them towards the purchase decision.

14.2.3 Closing Benefits

Closing **benefits** is ideal for clients who need extra motivation to commit. It focuses on highlighting the most relevant and urgent benefits for the customer, so that they feel that the value of the product or service is greater than any doubts they may have.

Steps to apply the benefit closing:
1. **Identify key benefits**: Choose those aspects that the customer valued most during the conversation.
2. **Highlight how the customer benefits immediately**: Make sure the customer understands how their post-purchase situation will improve.
3. **Invite the customer to take action to obtain the benefits**: Use language that invites immediate action, relating the benefits to the urgency of the purchase.

Example:
- Salesperson: "As we discussed, with this option, you will be able to reduce your operating costs by 20% from the first month. Do you think we start so that you start seeing these benefits right away?"

This closure is useful when the customer needs a compelling reason to act, and it helps highlight the value that the product or service will add to their situation.

14.2.4 Closing the incentive or closing the special offer

Closing **the incentive** is based on offering an additional benefit to motivate the customer to close the sale immediately. This incentive can be a discount, an additional service, free shipping, or any other added value that drives the customer to make a quick decision.

Steps to apply the incentive closure:
1. **Present the incentive as a limited offer**: Explain that the benefit is temporary, creating a sense of urgency.
2. **Relate the incentive to the customer's interests**: Make sure the incentive is something the customer would value, increasing its attractiveness.
3. **Invite the customer to take advantage of the offer**: Make the customer see the added value and advantage of acting immediately.

Example:
- Seller: "If you make the purchase today, we will offer you a 10% discount on the annual contract. It is an excellent opportunity to obtain the benefits of the service with additional savings. Would you like to take advantage of this offer?"

Closing the incentive is particularly effective for customers who show interest but need one last push to make the decision.

14.2.5 Test closure or warranty closure

For customers who are hesitant due to a lack of confidence in the product, the **test closure** or **warranty closure** offers them the ability to try the product risk-free or with the option to return if they are not satisfied. This gives them peace of mind and reduces the fear of making the wrong decision.

Steps to apply the test closure:
1. **Present the option of trial or warranty as a factor of trust**: Explain that the customer can experience the product without obligation.
2. **Detail the terms of the trial or warranty**: Make sure the customer understands how the trial works and what to expect if they decide not to proceed.
3. **Invite the customer to take advantage of the trial**: Highlight how the trial allows the customer to discover the value of the product without any risk.

Example:
- Salesperson: "I understand that you want to make sure it's the right choice. How about starting with a 30-day free trial? If for some reason you're not satisfied, you can cancel it without any charge."

Trial closure is a great option for hesitant customers, as it allows them to experience the product before fully committing, which increases confidence and reduces perceived risk.

14.2.6 Closing the abstract

Closing **the summary** is a technique that involves recapping the benefits, needs, and key points that the customer has expressed throughout the conversation. This technique is effective in helping the customer visualize how the product or service meets their specific needs and reaffirms their interest.

Steps to apply the summary closure:
1. **Recap the Key Points**: Highlight the most important aspects that have been discussed and that the client valued positively.
2. **Confirm the client's interest**: Verify that the client agrees with the points discussed and feels aligned with the proposal.
3. **Call to action**: Once the alignment is confirmed, invite the customer to proceed with the purchase.

Example:
- Salesperson: "So, we've talked about how this software will improve your efficiency and help you save time on daily tasks. In addition, it includes ongoing support and updates. Do you think we can proceed with the implementation so that you start to see these benefits?"

The closing of the summary allows the customer to see how the product fits perfectly with their needs, reinforcing the purchase decision.

14.3 Psychology of the sales closing: understanding customer behavior

Understanding the **psychology behind closing** allows salespeople to anticipate customer responses and apply the right technique at all times. Below are some key psychological principles that influence sales close success.

14.3.1 Principle of reciprocity
The principle of reciprocity suggests that customers tend to feel the need to reciprocate when they receive something of value, such as a discount or an additional service. This can be applied to the incentive technique or the special offer, creating a desire in the customer to repay the gesture with a purchase.

14.3.2 Scarcity principle
The scarcity principle indicates that customers tend to give more value to products or services when they perceive that they are available for a limited time. This principle is essential in special offer or incentive closings, since a limited period of time encourages decision-making.

14.3.3 Emotional alignment
Aligning the closing process with the client's values and emotions generates a feeling of trust and validation. Closures such as benefits or trial closings allow the salesperson to connect with the customer on an emotional level, generating a satisfactory closing.

14.3.4 Strengthening customer autonomy
The customer wants to feel like they're making an autonomous decision. Techniques such as alternative closing allow the client to have options and choice, which reinforces their perception of control and facilitates engagement.

14.4 Practical examples of Step-by-Step sales closing

Case study 1: Selling management software for SMEs
1. **Applied closure**: Incentive Closing
   - **Scenario**: The customer shows interest, but hesitation due to the price.
   - **Salesperson**: "I understand your concern about the budget. Today we have an offer with a 15% discount for contracting the annual package. It's an excellent opportunity to maximize value from the start. Would you like to take advantage of this special discount?"

Case study 2: Selling financial consulting services
1. **Applied Closure**: Alternative Closure
   - **Scenario**: The customer is undecided between two options.
   - **Salesperson**: "We can start with the basic package, which fits your current needs, or we can opt for the premium package, which includes monthly advice. Both are great options, which one do you prefer?"

Conclusion

Closing sales is a skill that, when mastered, allows salespeople to transform interest into engagement. Through techniques such as direct assumption closing, alternative closing, benefit closing, incentive closing, trial closing, and summary closing, salespeople can adapt to different types of customers and scenarios. Understanding the psychology of closing allows you to choose the right technique, creating a positive experience that closes the sale and lays the foundation for a lasting relationship with the customer.

Chapter 15

The importance of after-sales: Key to loyalty and long-term success

- "The seller's job doesn't end with the sale; After-sales service is what really creates long-term loyalty and retention."
  — *John Jantsch, "Duct Tape Selling"*

After-sales refers to all the activities and services that a company performs after having closed a sale. Although after-sales is often perceived as an add-on, it is actually an essential component of a comprehensive and effective sales strategy. Their goal is to maintain a positive relationship with the customer, ensure customer satisfaction, and build a solid foundation for loyalty. Aftersales not only contributes to customer retention, but also drives long-term growth through referrals and the possibility of upselling.

15.1 Customer loyalty: Beyond the initial sale

After-sales allows a company to stay in touch with the customer after the purchase, which contributes significantly to **loyalty**. When a customer perceives that the company is interested in their long-term satisfaction and not just the transaction, they are more likely to return in the future and become a repeat customer.

15.1.1 Importance of loyalty

Building customer loyalty is critical, as retention is much more cost-effective than acquiring new customers. Research suggests that acquiring a new customer can be five to seven times more expensive than retaining an existing one. In addition, loyal customers tend to spend more over time and are less sensitive to pricing.

15.1.2 How after-sales contributes to loyalty

Through after-sales activities such as follow-up, technical assistance, and ongoing support, the company can demonstrate that it cares about the customer and is committed to their success. This strengthens the relationship and increases the likelihood that the customer will choose the company again in the future.

15.2 Improve the customer experience: Ensure satisfaction and trust

Customer **experience** is a key factor that determines whether they will buy again or recommend the company to others. A well-managed after-sales service helps to identify and solve problems that the customer may have after the purchase, thus improving their experience and satisfaction.

15.2.1 Troubleshooting and technical support

It's common for problems or questions to arise after purchase, especially on products that require installation, setup, or maintenance. After-sales must ensure that the customer receives the help they need to maximize the value of their purchase.

15.2.2 Providing peace of mind

Offering warranty and support services not only helps resolve issues but also provides peace of mind to the customer as they know that the company is there to help them in case something goes wrong. This increases trust and improves the perception of the company.

15.3 Opportunities for upselling and cross-selling

After-sales offers multiple opportunities for **upselling** and **cross-selling**. Once a relationship of trust has been established, it is easier to offer complementary products or services that can meet new customer needs.

15.3.1 Identification of new needs

Continuous contact with the customer allows the company to detect new needs that may arise after the initial purchase. For example, if a customer purchases a security system, they may be interested in a monitoring service or an update in the future.

15.3.2 Building on established trust

Once the customer is satisfied with the product or service and has a good experience, they are more likely to trust the company for future purchases. Offering additional products or services at this stage may be more effective than doing so during the initial sale.

15.4 Encourage positive recommendations and testimonials

After-sales also plays an important role in **generating referrals** and obtaining **positive testimonials**. Satisfied customers are more likely to recommend the company to friends, family, and colleagues, which can result in organic growth and increased visibility in the market.

15.4.1 Importance of the recommendations

Referrals are one of the most effective ways to attract new customers, as they are backed by the trust that others have in those who make them. This reduces initial barriers and makes new customers feel more confident when considering the company.

15.4.2 How the aftermarket encourages recommendations

Post-purchase follow-up allows the company to measure customer satisfaction and, if satisfied, ask for a recommendation or testimonial. In addition, a good after-sales experience motivates the customer to share their experience in a natural way, which increases the credibility and reputation of the company.

15.5 Collecting Feedback for Continuous Improvement

After-sales is an excellent opportunity to **gather feedback** that allows the company to improve its products, services, and processes. Listening to the customer after the purchase provides valuable information that can help the company better adapt to the needs of the market.

15.5.1 Obtaining product information
Satisfaction surveys or after-sales interviews can reveal problems or areas for improvement in the product or service that might otherwise go unnoticed. This information is essential for innovation and to ensure that the product or service meets customer expectations.

15.5.2 Adjust marketing and sales strategies
By better understanding customer experiences and perceptions, the company can adjust its marketing and sales strategies to reflect the benefits that customers value most, or to preemptively address issues that may arise during the after-sales process.

15.6 Building a Long-Term relationship and competitive differentiation

In a competitive market, **differentiation** is key to standing out. After-sales is an area where businesses can differentiate themselves by delivering exceptional service that improves the customer experience significantly.

15.6.1 Strengthening the long-term relationship
The after-sales is the perfect opportunity to strengthen the relationship with the customer, making it easier to create a **long-term relationship** based on trust and commitment. By being present after the sale, the company demonstrates that it cares about the customer beyond immediate profit, which fosters loyalty.

15.6.2 Value Creation and Differentiation
Companies that offer excellent after-sales service are seen as more reliable and engaged, which can be a determining factor in customers choosing them over the competition. This approach also contributes to creating a perception of added value that goes beyond the simple transaction.

15.7 Strategies for effective after-sales

To implement effective after-sales, it is important to have a strategy that covers all stages of the process and is aligned with the company's objectives and customer expectations. Some key strategies include:

- **Active follow-up**: Contacting the customer shortly after purchase to check their satisfaction and answer any questions they may have.

- **Loyalty programs**: Offer incentives, discounts, or special benefits for recurring customers.
- **Technical Assistance and Support**: Provide high-quality support service to resolve technical issues quickly and effectively.
- **Satisfaction surveys**: Collect customer feedback and feedback to understand how they feel and how the experience can be improved.
- **Proactive communication**: Keeping the customer informed about updates, news and opportunities that may be of interest to them.

Conclusion

After-sales is a fundamental element that not only complements the sales process, but also strengthens the relationship with the customer and contributes to retention and loyalty. Through effective after-sales, businesses can improve the customer experience, get valuable recommendations, collect feedback for improvement, identify upsell opportunities, and create competitive differentiation. Ultimately, aftersales transforms satisfied customers into brand ambassadors, which is essential for the company's sustainable growth and long-term success.

Case study: After-sales follow-up for loyalty and sale of recommended - Sale of an HVAC system

In this case study, we will explore how to effectively track after-sales to build customer loyalty while also using their satisfaction to get sales through referrals. The product sold is an **intelligent air conditioning system**. The goal is to ensure that the customer is satisfied with their purchase and to build trust in them recommending the product to family or friends.

Case Context

Product: Smart HVAC system for the home, including automated temperature control, energy efficiency and connectivity to mobile devices.

Client: A family that has just installed the air conditioning system in their home to optimise comfort and reduce energy consumption.

Scenario: The company conducts after-sales follow-up to ensure customer satisfaction, resolve any issues, and request recommendations.

1. First follow-up contact: Satisfaction verification and resolution of doubts

The first after-sales contact should be made soon after installation, to verify that the customer is satisfied with the product and resolve any doubts they may have.

Action: Call the customer and ensure satisfaction
- **Salesperson**: "Hello, [Customer's Name]. I am [Your Name] from [Company Name]. I am contacting you to find out how your experience has been with the new HVAC system. Has everything worked out as I expected?"

Practical activity:
1. **Active Listening**: Pay attention to the customer's response and take note of any comments, questions, or issues they mention.
2. **Resolution of Doubts**: If the customer has any doubts or problems, solve them immediately or coordinate the necessary support to solve them.

Exercise:
- Write a script for a follow-up call where the customer has issues with system connectivity to their mobile device. Example: "I'm sorry to hear that you've had problems with connectivity. Let me walk you through a few steps to reconnect the system. If it doesn't work, we can schedule a technical visit to make sure it's working properly."

---

2. Ensure full customer satisfaction: solicit feedback and reinforce benefits

This step is key to confirming that the customer is satisfied and, if necessary, resolving any additional issues. In addition, it is an opportunity to remind the customer of the benefits of the product.

Action: Ask for feedback and reinforce benefits
- **Salesperson**: "We would like to know your opinion about the system. Have you noticed improvements in energy efficiency or in the comfort of your home? Remember that this system allows you to save up to 20% on your energy consumption, in addition to offering remote control from your cell phone. Have you had a chance to try that feature?"

Practical activity:
1. **Ask for specific feedback**: Ask the customer about specific aspects of the system, such as comfort, ease of use, or energy savings.
2. **Benefit reinforcement**: Remind the customer how the product helps them achieve their goals, highlighting the benefits they mentioned in the initial sale.

Exercise:
- **Write a series of questions** to get customer-specific feedback and reinforce benefits. Example: "Have you noticed a difference in the comfort of your home since the installation of the system? What did you think of the automatic temperature programming feature?"

3. Ask for a positive review or testimonial: Provide recommendations

Once customer satisfaction is confirmed, it's the right time to ask for a testimonial or review. Not only does this help the company improve its reputation, but it also prepares the customer to make recommendations to others.

Action: Ask for a review or testimonial
- **Salesperson:** "We are very happy to hear that you are satisfied with the system. It would help us a lot if you could share your experience. Would you like to leave a review on our website or give us a testimonial? This will help other people learn more about our product and service."

Practical activity:
1. **Ask for a friendly testimonial:** Make the request in a friendly way and explain to the customer how they can help others with their experience.
2. **Offer review assistance:** If the customer seems willing, offer to send them a direct link or guide to make leaving the review easy and quick.

Exercise:
- **Write a script to ask for a review or testimonial**, including a brief explanation of why it's important. Example: "Your feedback is very valuable to us and other potential customers. With a brief review, you can help us improve and guide others interested in our products. Would you like to receive a link to share your experience?"

4. Ask for recommendations: Turn satisfaction into new sales opportunities

If the customer has expressed satisfaction, it is a good opportunity to ask them to recommend the product to their family, friends or colleagues. This can be done directly, or through a referral benefit offer.

Action: Ask for recommendations with an incentive
- **Salesperson:** "We're happy you're enjoying your new system. If you know anyone else who could benefit from an HVAC system like this, we'd love to hear from you. In fact, we offer an incentive for every customer you refer to us. Would you like to learn more about how our referral program works?"

Practical activity:
1. **Ask for recommendations naturally**: Make asking for recommendations feel like a natural extension of the conversation, based on their satisfaction.
2. **Offer referral incentives**: Explain the benefits the customer can get by recommending the product to others.

Exercise:
- **Write a script to ask for a referral** and include an incentive. Example: "If you know someone who is interested in improving the energy efficiency of their home, please feel free to refer us. In addition, we offer a discount on your next purchase for each successful referral. Would you like to know the details?"

5. Appreciation and ongoing follow-up: Cultivating the relationship for future sales

Finally, after asking for recommendations, it is important to thank the customers and assure them that they can count on the company's support in the long term. This cultivates a long-lasting relationship and creates opportunities for future sales or upgrades.

Action: Be thankful and keep in touch
- **Salesperson**: "Thank you so much for your time and for sharing your experience with us. We're happy to hear that you're enjoying your new system. We will be here for any questions or needs you may have in the future, and we will also be informing you about updates and new offers. Thank you again for your trust."

Practical activity:
1. **Genuine appreciation**: Demonstrates gratitude for the customer's time and willingness.
2. **Offer future support**: Make sure the customer knows how to contact the company for support and mention sending information about new offers.

Exercise:
- **Write a closing message** that includes a thank you and offers ongoing support. Example: "We really appreciate that you have trusted us for your HVAC system. Remember that we are here for any questions you have, and don't hesitate to call us if you need help. We will keep you updated on developments that may be of interest to you."

Case Study Conclusion

In this case study, the steps of effective after-sales follow-up to ensure customer satisfaction, get a recommendation, and foster a long-term relationship have been covered. Through these activities, the customer experience is improved, loyalty is increased, and opportunities for additional sales are opened through referrals. After-sales, when carefully and proactively managed, not only strengthens the relationship with the customer, but also becomes a source of growth and new business opportunities.

Chapter 16

The importance of care and after-sales customer service

- "A well-served customer is the best ambassador for a brand. Customer service is the cornerstone of a long-lasting relationship."
— Ken Blanchard, "The One Minute Manager"

Customer **care and service** are essential components to any successful sales and after-sales strategy. Not only do these elements ensure customer satisfaction after the sale, but they are also critical to building long-lasting relationships and building loyalty. In this chapter, we will explore in depth how quality customer service and attention contribute to customer satisfaction, loyalty, and retention, and how they can become a key competitive advantage for any business. In addition, strategies and practical examples will be presented to offer exceptional customer service in the after-sales.

16.1 Customer service as a pillar of after-sales

Customer service doesn't end with the sale; In fact, in many cases, it is in the after-sales stage when the quality of the relationship with the customer is defined. Through continuous and quality service, the company can keep the customer satisfied, increase their loyalty and ensure that they get the maximum value from the product or service purchased.

16.1.1 Definition of customer support
Customer **service** encompasses all the interactions a customer has with a company before, during, and after the purchase. It refers to the way the company responds to customer needs, queries, and problems, ensuring that their experience is positive and satisfying.

16.1.2 Role of customer service in after-sales
In the after-sales sector, customer service fulfills key functions such as:

- **Problem solving**: Addresses any issues the customer may experience with the product or service.
- **Support and advice**: Provides additional information and guidance to the customer on how to maximize the use of the product.
- **Satisfaction reinforcement**: Through continuous interactions, the company ensures that the customer is satisfied and that their expectations are met.

16.1.3 Impact of customer service on loyalty
Quality after-sales customer service strengthens customer confidence in the company and increases the likelihood that they will buy again in the future. Satisfied customers are more likely to recommend the company and become brand ambassadors, which broadens the company's reach and strengthens its reputation.

16.2 Key components of good customer service in the after-sales

To provide exceptional after-sales customer service, it's important to focus on certain critical components that contribute to a positive and memorable experience.

16.2.1 Empathy and active listening
Empathy and **active listening** are essential skills in customer service. These qualities allow the representative to understand the customer's

concerns and needs, creating an emotional connection that facilitates problem-solving and builds trust.
- **Empathy**: It is about putting yourself in the customer's shoes and understanding their feelings and frustrations.
- **Active listening**: It involves paying attention to what the customer says, as well as their emotions and tone of voice, to capture their needs beyond words.

16.2.2 Efficiency and rapid problem resolution

Customers value having their issues resolved quickly and efficiently. This requires **in-depth knowledge of the product or service** and the ability to provide accurate solutions without unnecessary delays. A quick resolution is critical to prevent customer frustration and to ensure that their experience remains positive.

16.2.3 Clear and transparent communication

Clear **and transparent communication** is critical to ensure that the customer understands every step of the process and knows what to expect. This includes explaining in a simple way the procedures, wait times and any additional costs that may arise.

16.2.4 Proactivity and monitoring

Good customer service isn't just about answering queries or solving problems; it also involves being **proactive** in following up with the customer to check on their satisfaction. This can include making follow-up calls, sending emails with additional instructions, or asking if there's anything else the company can help with.

16.3 Strategies for offering exceptional after-sales service

Implementing a quality after-sales service requires a strategic approach and a series of key practices that guarantee a satisfactory customer experience.

16.3.1 Offer multi-channel support channels

It's important for customers to have multiple support channels available, such as phone, email, online chat, and social media. This way, they can choose the most convenient means of getting help. Multichannel **service** increases accessibility and facilitates customer contact with the company.

16.3.2 Service customization

Personalizing customer service means tailoring service to each customer's specific needs. This may involve using your name, remembering details of previous interactions, and providing solutions that fit your particular situation.

16.3.3 Use of technology to improve service

Technology plays a key role in customer service. Tools such as **customer relationship management (CRM) systems, chatbot,** and **automated satisfaction surveys** allow the company to provide efficient and personalized service.

16.3.4 Continuous training of personnel

Quality after-sales service depends on a trained staff who understand both the product and customer service best practices. Ongoing **training** ensures that the team is up to date with the latest customer service updates and techniques, allowing them to offer the best possible support.

16.4 The importance of satisfaction of the customer in the after-sales

Customer satisfaction is one of the most important indicators of after-sales effectiveness. Not only does a satisfied customer have a positive experience, but they're also more likely to buy again and recommend the company to others.

16.4.1 Measuring customer satisfaction

To assess satisfaction, it is essential to implement measurement tools, such as:

- **Satisfaction surveys**: They allow the customer to rate their experience and offer feedback.
- **Net Promoter Score (NPS):** Measures how likely the customer is to recommend the company to others.
- **Feedback analysis**: Evaluating customer feedback allows you to identify areas for improvement and opportunities for growth.

16.4.2 Importance of feedback

Feedback is essential to understanding customer perceptions and making adjustments that improve the overall experience. Listening to the customer and acting on their feedback shows that the company values their opinion and is committed to continuous improvement.

16.5 How to turn after-sales into a competitive advantage

Exceptional after-sales service can be a powerful **competitive advantage** that differentiates a company in the market. Customers value good after-sales service more than a low price, and they are likely to choose a company that offers superior service, even if their prices are slightly higher.

16.5.1 Building customer loyalty and retention
After-sales contributes significantly to **customer loyalty**. Not only does a loyal customer return for additional purchases, but they are also more tolerant of problems and more willing to wait for solutions. Loyalty, in turn, reduces customer acquisition costs and contributes to sustained growth.

16.5.2 Differentiation through the Service
A quality after-sales service is not common in all companies, so those who implement it manage to stand out. By offering an outstanding after-sales experience, businesses can differentiate themselves from the competition and become the customer's preferred choice.

16.6 Care case studies and after-sales customer service

To illustrate the importance of customer service and attention in after-sales, here are some practical examples that show how to implement these strategies to achieve customer satisfaction and loyalty.

Case study 1: Proactive follow-up to ensure satisfaction
A company that sells home appliances follows up with each customer one week after the product is delivered. During this follow-up, ask if the customer is satisfied and if they have had any problems. If any problem is detected, a technician is sent to the home to solve it.

- **Result**: The customer perceives that the company cares about their experience and feels more willing to recommend it to others.

Case study 2: Using technology to improve service
A software company uses a CRM to record every customer interaction. This allows any support representative to view the customer's history and offer personalized attention. If the customer needs help, the representative can offer a quick solution tailored to their needs.

- **Result**: The customer feels that their problem is important and that they receive a specific solution, which increases their satisfaction and likelihood of buying again.

Case study 3: Referral incentives after exceptional service

A financial services company offers incentives to its satisfied customers to recommend the company to friends and family. At the same time, she ensures that each client receives a high-quality, personalized service, so that they are motivated to recommend her.

- **Result**: The company not only builds loyalty with its existing customers, but also expands its customer base through referrals.

16.7 Measurement and continuous improvement of after-sales service

To maintain a high-quality after-sales service, it is essential to measure and analyze the performance of the service and make continuous adjustments that allow the customer experience to be improved.

16.7.1 Main evaluation metrics

Some of the key metrics for evaluating after-sales service include:
- **Response time**: How long it takes for the company to respond to a customer request or issue.
- **Resolution time**: How quickly the issue is fixed once the customer has been contacted.
- **Customer Satisfaction Index (CSAT)**: Measures the customer's overall satisfaction with the service.

16.7.2 Feedback-based settings

Customer feedback should be used to identify patterns and areas for improvement. By making continuous adjustments based on this information, the company can ensure that its after-sales service evolves and adapts to changing customer expectations.

Conclusion

Customer service and attention in the after-sales service are essential to achieve customer satisfaction, loyalty and retention. Through a strategic and continuous focus on after-sales, companies can strengthen the relationship with their customers, obtain recommendations, and differentiate themselves in the market. Investing in quality after-sales service not only increases the value perceived by the customer, but also contributes to the long-term success and growth of the company. Ultimately, after-sales is not only the end of the sales process, but also the beginning of a long-lasting and trusting relationship between the customer and the company.

Chapter 17

Retention strategies and reactivation of customers in sales

- "Customer retention is not a luxury, it's a necessity. Loyal customers are the most valuable asset a company can have."
— *Frederick F. Reichheld, "The Loyalty Effect"*

Retaining existing customers and reviving those who have stopped buying are essential strategies to ensure a company's long-term growth and sustainability. **Customer retention** refers to the actions a business takes to keep its customers active and satisfied, fostering loyalty, and preventing them from migrating to competitors. Customer **reactivation**, on the other hand, focuses on recovering those customers who have reduced or abandoned their relationship with the company. This chapter explores best practices and strategies for retaining and reactivating customers, as well as the importance of measuring the effectiveness of these actions and their impact on the business.

17.1 The importance of customer retention

Retaining customers is critical to the success of any business, as acquiring a new customer can cost five to seven times more than keeping an existing one. In addition, loyal customers tend to spend more and become brand ambassadors. Below are the main reasons why customer retention is key to business sustainability.

17.1.1 Cost efficiency in retention vs. acquisition

The cost of retaining a customer is significantly less than the cost of acquiring a new one. Companies that invest in retention enjoy higher returns, as returning customers tend to buy more frequently and spend more over time. This increase in loyalty reduces the need for constant investments in advertising and customer acquisition campaigns, allowing the company to maximize its budget.

17.1.2 Increasing Customer Lifetime Value (CLV)

Customer Lifetime Value (CLV) is a metric that measures the total economic value of a customer throughout their relationship with the company. By retaining customers longer, the company increases CLV, which translates into higher revenue in the long run. A loyal customer is more likely to make additional purchases, try new products or services, and pay a premium price because of the trust they have developed in the company.

17.1.3 Creating brand ambassadors

Satisfied and loyal customers not only generate recurring revenue, but also promote the brand through referrals. These **brand ambassadors** influence other people's purchase decisions, as their opinions are often perceived as more trustworthy than conventional advertising. Customer retention encourages this behavior, increasing brand visibility and attracting new customers through **word-of-mouth marketing**.

17.2 Customer retention strategies

To retain customers, companies must implement strategies that allow them to maintain their interest and satisfaction over time. These strategies range from personalizing the customer experience to creating loyalty programs.

17.2.1 Customer experience personalization

Personalization is one of the most effective strategies for improving the customer experience and fostering retention. By tailoring communication, offers, and service to each customer's individual preferences, the company demonstrates that it values their relationship and strives to meet their specific needs.

- **Customer segmentation**: Identify customer segments and adapt marketing and communication strategies to each group, based on their characteristics and behaviors.
- **Personalized recommendations**: Use information about the customer's purchase history and preferences to offer products or services that align with their interests.

17.2.2 Loyalty programs

Loyalty **programs** reward customers for their loyalty and give them incentives to continue shopping from the company. These programs may include reward points, exclusive discounts, access to products before they are released, or free services.

- **Point system**: Customers accumulate points with each purchase, which they can then redeem for products, discounts, or other benefits.
- **Membership levels**: By establishing membership levels (e.g., bronze, silver, and gold), the company incentivizes customers to reach the next level, offering additional benefits as they increase their purchases.

17.2.3 Continuous and proactive communication

Maintaining **constant communication** with customers helps to strengthen the relationship and keep them informed about news, offers and changes in products or services. Proactive communication is key to preventing dissatisfaction and ensuring that the customer feels valued.

- **Personalized newsletters**: Send regular emails that include customer-relevant content, such as product recommendations, company news, or special events.
- **After-sales follow-up**: Follow up after the sale to make sure the customer is satisfied and resolve any issues.

17.2.4 Quality Customer Care and Support

Efficient **and accessible customer support** is essential to retaining customers. The company must ensure that the customer can get help quickly when they need it, and that the service they receive is courteous, professional, and effective.

- **Multi-channel support**: Provide different contact options, such as phone, online chat, email, and social media, so that the customer can choose the channel they prefer.
- **Staff training**: Ensuring that the support team is trained to resolve issues quickly and provide a positive customer experience.

17.3 Reactivation of inactive customers

This is a strategy that seeks to recover those who have stopped buying or have decreased their purchase frequency. There are several reasons why a customer may become inactive, such as dissatisfaction, change in needs, or simple forgetfulness. Reactivating these customers allows them to take advantage of their previous knowledge of the brand and increase profitability without the need to acquire new customers.

17.3.1 Identification of inactive customers
The first step in reactivating inactive customers is to identify them. This can be done by analyzing sales data and buying patterns. Once identified, they can be classified according to their level of inactivity and their potential value to the company.

- **Purchase frequency analysis**: Determine how many days have passed since the customer's last purchase and define criteria to classify customers as inactive.
- **Customer value**: Evaluate the customer's purchase history to determine their potential value and prioritize those that could generate a higher return.

17.3.2 Sending personalized offers and reminders
Personalized **reminders** and **offers** are effective tools to attract the attention of inactive customers and motivate them to return. These offers may include discounts, exclusive promotions, or invitations to special events.

- **Re-engagement campaigns**: Send personalized emails that remind the customer of the brand's benefits and offer special incentives to return.
- **Welcome back offers**: Offer discounts or welcome gifts for those customers who return to shop after a period of inactivity.

17.3.3 Surveys and feedback to understand the reason for inactivity
To understand why a customer became inactive, it's helpful to conduct surveys or ask for feedback. This allows you to identify issues that may have led to downtime and take steps to improve the customer experience.

- **Return** surveys: Ask the customer about their past experience and reasons why they stopped buying, using that information to adjust retention strategies.
- **Feedback interviews**: For high-value clients, conduct phone interviews that delve into their needs and expectations.

17.3.4 Improving customer experience based on feedback

Feedback obtained through surveys and interviews should be used to make adjustments to products, services, or processes that may have caused customer downtime. Not only does this help win back customers, but it also improves the overall experience for everyone.

17.4 Measuring success of retention and reactivation strategies

To evaluate the effectiveness of retention and reactivation strategies, it is critical to measure results and analyze data. Some key metrics include:

- **Customer retention rate**: Measures the percentage of customers who are still active after a given period, indicating the success of retention strategies.
- **Customer reactivation rate**: Measures the percentage of inactive customers who repurchase after implementing reactivation strategies.
- **Customer Lifetime Value (CLV):** Measures the total economic value of a customer throughout their relationship with the company. An increase in CLV indicates success in retention and reactivation.
- **Churn rate**: Measures the percentage of customers who stop buying or canceling services. A reduction in this rate suggests an improvement in retention strategies.

17.5 Customer retention and reactivation use cases

Case study 1: Retention through loyalty programs

An online store implements a points system that rewards customers for every purchase. As they accumulate points, they can redeem them for discounts or exclusive products. The store also sends personalized reminders to customers about the number of points they have available and opportunities to redeem them.

- **Result**: Customers feel valued and motivated to keep shopping to accumulate more points, which increases retention and strengthens loyalty.

Case study 2: Reactivation through exclusive offers

A subscription services company detects that some of its customers have canceled or reduced their subscriptions. To win back these customers, the company sends a personalized offer that includes a discount on the first bill if they reactivate their subscription within the month.

- **Result**: A significant percentage of customers decide to reactivate their subscription, attracted by the savings and the opportunity to enjoy the service again.

Case study 3: Feedback to improve customer experience

A telecommunications company conducts satisfaction surveys among its inactive customers to understand the reasons for their churn. You find that most customers were frustrated by the wait time at support. The company takes steps to improve wait times and communicates changes to inactive customers.

- **Result**: Customers notice the improvement and some decide to reactivate their service, satisfied with the company's response to their needs.

Conclusion

Customer retention and reactivation are key strategies for the long-term success of any business. Through personalized techniques and a focus on customer experience, businesses can keep their customers active and satisfied, as well as win back those who have stopped buying. Implementing a strong strategy not only increases customer lifetime value, but also reduces acquisition costs and contributes to sustainable, profitable growth.

Chapter 18

Practical sales exercises for real situations

Hands-on exercises are critical for salespeople, as it allows them to develop and hone their skills in a safe environment, with the opportunity to receive feedback and learn from their experiences. Through simulations, role-playing, and performance evaluations, salespeople can practice and refine techniques, and prepare to face real-life sales situations; improving their ability to identify needs, handle objections, close sales, and ensure customer satisfaction and loyalty.

Below are a series of practical sales exercises that can be applied in real situations.

1. Sales simulation exercise:
Tangible and intangible product scenarios

This exercise is designed for participants to practice the entire sales process, from initial contact to closing, using different types of products: a tangible one (e.g., an appliance) and an intangible one (such as a consulting service). It is based on real scenarios and allows you to develop skills to identify customer needs, overcome objections, and use closing techniques.

Instructions:
1. **Assign roles**: Divide participants into pairs, with one assuming the role of salesperson and the other of customer.
2. **Define the product or service**: Assign each pair a tangible and an intangible product. For example, an appliance and a financial advisory service.
3. **Sales scenario**: Provide each customer with a fictitious profile with interests, needs, and potential objections related to the product or service. Salespeople should adapt to this profile and use sales techniques to address objections and close the sale.
4. **Performance evaluation**: After each simulation, participants should discuss strengths and areas for improvement in the sales process. You can assign an observer to provide additional feedback.

Step-by-step for the sales simulation exercise

Step 1: Preparing the exercise
1. **Divide participants into pairs:**
    - Organize the participants into pairs, where one will assume the role of salesperson and the other the role of customer.
    - If you have a large group, you can assign an observer to each pair to take notes and provide feedback.

2. **Select the product or service:**
    - Assign each pair two types of products: one tangible and one intangible.
    - **Example of a tangible product**: An appliance such as a high-end refrigerator.
    - **Example of an intangible product**: A financial advisory service.
    - Make sure each pair has a basic profile of the product or service, including features, benefits, and price.

Step 2: Define the sales scenario
1. **Create a customer profile:**
   - Provide them with a fictitious profile with interests, needs, and possible objections.
   - **Example profile for tangible products**: A customer who is looking for an efficient refrigerator, but is also concerned about the initial cost.
   - **Example profile for intangible products**: A client who is interested in investing in the future, but has doubts about the risks and profitability.

2. **Establish the sales environment:**
   - Define whether the sale is made in a physical store, in a video call, or in a consulting office.
   - Clarify the environment so that salespeople adjust to the particularities of each situation (e.g., body language in a store, or visual presentations on a video call).

Step 3: Perform the simulation
1. **Start of the simulation:**
   - Instruct salespeople to start with a greeting and a friendly introduction.
   - The goal is to establish a connection and begin to discover the customer's needs through open-ended questions.

2. **Identification of needs:**
   - The salesperson should ask questions to discover the customer's needs, motivations, and any objections or concerns they may have.
   - **Example question**: "What features do you consider most important to the product?" or "What would you like to achieve with this service?"

3. **Presentation of the product or service:**
   - Based on the information obtained, the salesperson should tailor their presentation to highlight the benefits that best meet the customer's needs.
   - **For the tangible product**: Explain how the refrigerator's features fit the customer's expectations for efficiency.
   - **For the intangible product**: Explain how the financial advisory service can help the client achieve their investment goals.

4. **Handling objections:**
    - The client must submit a specific objection based on the assigned profile.
    - The salesperson must respond effectively, using techniques such as reframing, storytelling, or using data and evidence to address the customer's concern.
    - **Example of objection:** "I'm not sure if it's worth making this investment now."
    - **Seller's response:** "I understand your doubts. In fact, many customers shared that concern at first, but after a few months, they tell us that they are happy with the savings they have achieved. Would you like us to review some ROI data together?"

5. **Closing of the sale:**
    - The salesperson should try to close the sale using a closing technique appropriate to the customer's profile and product type.
    - **Closing example:** "We can start with the basic investment package, which allows you to grow your capital with moderate risk. Would you like to start with this option?"

Step 4: Performance evaluation
1. **Feedback between salespeople and customers:**
    - Once the simulation is complete, the customer shares their experience with the salesperson, discussing what worked well and any areas where the salesperson could improve.

2. **Observer takes notes and provides feedback:**
    - If there are observers, they should share their impressions, mentioning aspects such as handling objections, using closure techniques, and the ability to identify needs.
    - Each observer can use a checklist to evaluate points such as tone, clarity in presentation, and response to objections.

Step 5: Group discussion and final reflection
1. **Group reflection and discussion:**
    - Gather all the pairs and ask them to share their experiences, including the challenges they faced and the techniques they used.
    - Discuss which strategies were effective and why and allow participants to learn from their peers' experiences.

2. **Analysis of areas for improvement**:
    - Ask participants about what they would improve in future interactions and what their key learning points are.
    - Discuss with the group the importance of adaptation in the sales process and how each customer can present different challenges.

Objective:
This exercise helps salespeople practice adapting their approach based on the type of product and customer profile, developing skills to identify needs and overcome objections.

2. Role-Playing Exercise: Handling Objections

Role-playing is an excellent technique to practice how to handle objections and strengthen the responsiveness of salespeople. In this exercise, participants should practice how to respond to common objections that customers often raise during the sales process.

Instructions:
1. **Select objection scenarios**: Choose a few common objections, such as "the price is too high," "I'm not sure if I need it now," or "I need to consult with someone else."
2. **Assign roles**: One participant assumes the role of salesperson and another that of customer. The customer must raise the assigned objection, and the salesperson must respond appropriately.
3. **Practice response techniques**: The salesperson should apply different techniques to handle objections, such as positive reframing, storytelling, or the use of data and evidence.
4. **Role rotation**: Change roles so that all participants have the opportunity to practice as both salespeople and customers.
5. **Evaluation**: After each simulation, participants should analyze the effectiveness of the responses, identifying points for improvement and suggestions for refining objection handling techniques.

Step by step for the role-playing exercise: handling objections

Step 1: Preparing the exercise
1. **Define the group and roles**:
    - Divide the participants into pairs, where one will assume the role of **salesperson** and the other the role of **customer**.

- If you have a large group, designate an **additional observer** to take notes and provide feedback.
2. **Select common objections:**
   - Prepare a list of common objections that customers often raise in the sales process.
   - **Examples of common objections:**
     - "The price is too high."
     - "I'm not sure I need it now."
     - "I need to consult with someone else."
     - "I don't know the brand and prefer something with more reputation."
3. **Assign an objection to each pair:**
   - Give each customer an objection from the list. Alternatively, it allows customers to choose an objection so that the salesperson doesn't know about it in advance, which adds realism to the exercise.

Step 2: Instructions for participants
1. **Instructions for the seller:**
   - The salesperson should address the customer's objection using objection handling techniques, such as positive reframing, the use of testimonials, storytelling, or presenting data and evidence.
   - The salesperson is encouraged to be flexible and adapt their response to the customer's situation and tone.

2. **Customer Instructions:**
   - The client must raise the assigned objection and behave realistically, showing interest, but also questions or doubts.
   - The customer can respond to the salesperson's answers, asking additional questions for the salesperson to practice deepening and adapting their answers.

3. **Instructions for the observer:**
   - If there is an observer, their task is to take notes on the interaction, including the clarity and effectiveness of the salesperson's response, their tone and body language, and the empathy shown to the customer.
   - The observer should be prepared to give objective and constructive feedback after the simulation is completed.

Step 3: Role-playing
1. **Start of the simulation:**
   - The salesperson starts the conversation, introducing the product or service and inviting the customer to express their doubts or concerns.
   - The customer presents the assigned objection in a natural and clear way, indicating why he has doubts about the purchase.

2. **Seller's response to objection:**
   - The salesperson should address the customer's objection strategically, using a technique they feel is appropriate.
   - **Examples of objection handling techniques:**
     - **Positive framing:** "I understand that the price may seem high, but it also includes extended warranty and 24/7 technical support, which is a long-term investment."
     - **Storytelling:** "I remember another client who was initially hesitant about the price, but after seeing the savings he achieved, he told us that it was the best decision. Would you like to hear more about your experience?"
     - **Social Proof:** "Most of our customers have had very positive results with this product, and more than 90% have given us a 5-star rating for quality. Would you like to see some testimonials?"

3. **Interaction and deepening:**
   - The customer can ask additional questions or show reservations about the seller's response, allowing the seller to deepen their technique and strengthen their arguments.
   - It is recommended that the seller ask questions to verify that they have resolved the objection or to get more details about the customer's concerns.

Step 4: Evaluation and Feedback
1. **Exchange of impressions between seller and customer:**
   - After the simulation, the customer should provide feedback to the salesperson about their perception of the interaction. This includes what you considered effective and any suggestions for improvement.

2. **Feedback from the observer (if applicable):**
   - The observer provides a detailed assessment, highlighting key aspects such as empathy, clarity, the effectiveness of the technique used, and how objections were addressed.
   - You can use a checklist that includes:
     - **Clarity in the answer**: Was it clear and easy to understand?
     - **Empathy**: Did you show understanding towards the customer's concerns?
     - **Effectiveness in the technique**: Was the objection handling technique appropriate for the situation?
     - **Adaptation**: Was the salesperson's response adjusted to the customer's reactions?

3. **Role rotation:**
   - Change the roles of salesperson and customer, assigning new objections. This allows each participant to practice both the role of salesperson and customer and address different types of objections.

Step 5: Group discussion and final reflection
1. **Group discussion:**
   - Once all the pairs have finished, gather the group to discuss the techniques they found most effective and those that proved challenging.
   - Ask participants which technique worked best for them and how they felt responding to objections.

2. **Reflection on areas for improvement:**
   - Ask salespeople to share any difficulties they faced and how they could improve their response in the future.
   - He discusses the importance of adaptability and empathy in handling objections, highlighting that each client is unique and requires a personalized approach.

Objective:
This role-playing exercise allows participants to practice and hone their skills to handle objections effectively, building confidence and fluency in real sales situations. The feedback received during the activity helps salespeople to better understand their strengths and identify areas for improvement, increasing their preparedness and responsiveness to customer objections.

3. Sales Performance evaluation exercise: sales closing role-playing

The closing of sales is a critical stage and mastering it is essential. In this exercise, participants will practice different closing techniques, evaluating their performance and effectiveness in simulated situations.

Instructions:
1. **Define Closing Techniques**: Provide a list of closing techniques, such as Alternative Closing, Profit Closing, Incentive Closing, and Test Closing.
2. **Sales scenario**: Assign a product or service and a customer profile to each participant.
3. **Closing simulation**: The salesperson must choose and apply a closing technique that he or she considers appropriate for the customer's profile. The customer can accept or raise additional objections.
4. **Evaluation**: After each simulation, the observer (or group) should analyze the closing technique used, assessing the clarity, confidence, and ability of the salesperson to ensure customer engagement.
5. **Feedback**: At the end, the salesperson should receive feedback on their performance, highlighting the positive aspects and areas for improvement.

Step by step for the role-playing exercise: Sales closing

Step 1: Preparing the exercise
1. **Define the group and roles**:
   - Divide the participants into pairs, assigning one the role of **salesperson** and the other the role of **customer**.
   - If you have a large group, include an **observer** who will take notes and provide feedback at the end of the exercise.

2. **Select and explain closure techniques**:
   - Before you begin, review some of the main closure techniques that will be practiced. Provide a brief description of each one for participants to keep in mind.
   - **Examples of closure techniques**:
     - **Alternative closing**: Offer two options for the customer to choose the one that best suits them.
     - **Benefits closing**: Summarize the key benefits the client will receive, motivating them to take action.
     - **Incentive closing**: Offer an additional incentive, such as a discount, to motivate immediate purchase.

- **Trial closing**: Suggest a free or low-cost trial for the customer to experience the product or service.

3. **Assign a product or service and the customer's profile**:
   - Provide a product or service to each couple, along with a basic customer profile that includes needs, interests, and potential objections.
   - **Product example**: A management software for small businesses.
   - **Customer profile example**: An entrepreneur looking to improve efficiency, but who is concerned about cost and implementation time.

Step 2: Instructions for participants
1. **Instructions for the seller**:
   - The seller must use the closing techniques provided to try to close the sale.
   - During the simulation, you should recognize the customer's buying signals and respond in an adapted way to their comments and objections, if they arise.
2. **Customer instructions**:
   - The customer must interact in a natural way, showing interest, but also asking questions or doubts. It can simulate behaviors that indicate both indecision and willingness to close.
   - If the salesperson does not detect a buy signal or uses an inappropriate technique, the customer may express hesitation for the salesperson to try another technique.
3. **Instructions for the observer (if applicable)**:
   - The observer should take notes on the interaction, including how the salesperson applies closing techniques, how they respond to customer cues, and how they adapt their approach.
   - The observer should be prepared to provide constructive feedback, focusing on the clarity, confidence, and effectiveness of the closure technique used.

Step 3: Performing the sales closing role-playing
1. **Start of the simulation**:
   - The salesperson begins the interaction with a brief presentation of the product or service and a confirmation of the customer's interests and needs.
   - You should prepare the ground for closing, highlighting the key benefits and assessing the customer's level of interest.

2. **Application of the closure technique:**
   - Based on the customer's information and reactions, the salesperson selects a closing technique suitable for the situation.
   - **Application examples:**
     - **Alternative closure:** "We can proceed with the standard plan which is more affordable, or with the premium plan which includes advanced technical support. Which one do you think is best?"
     - **Closing benefits:** "We've talked about how this software can improve your efficiency and reduce costs. How about we implement it so that you start seeing these benefits soon?"
     - **Incentive Closure:** "If you confirm the purchase today, we can offer you a 10% discount in the first year. Would you like to take advantage of this offer?"
     - **Test closure:** "I understand that you want to make sure that it is the right choice. How about starting with a 30-day free trial?"

3. **Interaction and adaptation:**
   - The customer may respond with signs of acceptance or, on the contrary, present an objection or express doubts.
   - The salesperson must be flexible and be prepared to adjust their approach according to the customer's reaction, reinforcing the closing technique or using another one if necessary.

Step 4: Evaluation and feedback

1. **Feedback between salesperson and customer:**
   - At the end of the simulation, the client provides their opinion on the closing technique used, indicating what worked well and what aspects could have been handled differently.

2. **Observer assessment (if applicable):**
   - The observer shares their notes and comments on the interaction, pointing out aspects such as:
     - **Clarity and confidence:** Was the salesperson clear in their message and demonstrated confidence in applying the technique?
     - **Adaptation:** Did the salesperson adjust to the customer's reactions?

- **Closing efficiency**: Was the closing technique suitable for the customer's profile and the product or service?

3. **Role rotation**:
    - Switch roles so that all participants have the opportunity to practice both the closing and the client role.
    - Assign new products and customer profiles to practice with different scenarios.

Step 5: Group discussion and final reflection
1. **Group discussion**:
    - After everyone has participated, gather the group to discuss the closure techniques that worked best and those that presented challenges.
    - Allow participants to share their impressions and learnings, and discuss which techniques are best suited to certain types of clients.

2. **Reflection on the use of closure**:
    - It invites sellers to reflect on how they can improve the detection of buy signals and how to select the most appropriate closing technique in each situation.
    - Remember that closing is a combination of strategy and sensitivity towards the customer, and highlights the importance of constant practice.

Objective:
This exercise focuses on helping participants practice sales closing techniques in simulated situations. Through role-playing, salespeople can rehearse different strategies to close a sale, receive feedback on their performance, and improve their ability to secure customer engagement. This exercise focuses on the ability to recognize the right moment and apply the most effective closing technique.

3. After-sales follow-up simulation exercise: Thank you call and collect feedback

This exercise focuses on after-sales follow-up, a crucial step in ensuring customer satisfaction, strengthening the relationship, and fostering loyalty. During the exercise, participants will practice how to make a thank you call and how to collect customer feedback. This type of follow-up allows any concerns to be resolved and promotes future recommendations or additional sales.

Instructions:
1. **Assign roles and scenarios**: Assign the salesperson role to one participant and the customer role to another. Provide a scenario where the customer has just purchased a product or service.
2. **Make the follow-up call**: The seller should call the customer to thank them for the purchase and ask them about their experience, inviting them to share their opinion and any problems that may have arisen.
3. **Respond to feedback**: If the customer has a concern or problem, the salesperson should demonstrate empathy, offer solutions, and confirm their satisfaction.
4. **Encourage referrals**: At the end of the call, the salesperson should take the opportunity to ask for a referral or invite the customer to refer the company to others.
5. **Evaluation and feedback**: Analyze the pitch, empathy, and ability of the salesperson to build trust and solve problems. Observers should provide constructive feedback.

Step by step for the after-sales follow-up exercise

Step 1: Preparing the exercise
1. **Define the group and roles**:
   - Form pairs of participants, assigning one the role of **salesperson** and the other the role of **customer**.
   - If the group is large, include an **observer** to take notes and provide feedback at the end of the simulation.

2. **Assign a product or service and a customer profile**:
   - Provide each pair with a recently purchased product or service and a customer profile, including details such as their expected level of satisfaction, motivations, and potential doubts.
   - **Product example**: A home security system.
   - **Customer profile example**: A customer who valued the recommendation of friends and is looking to improve the security of their home, but is concerned about the complexity of the installation.

3. **Define the goal of the call**:
   - The call has three objectives: to thank the customer for their purchase, to verify their satisfaction and to collect feedback to improve the service.
   - Optionally, you can add a referral request, depending on how the conversation progresses.

Step 2: Instructions for participants
1. **Instructions for the seller:**
   - The salesperson should make the call starting with a thank you and check in on how the customer's experience has been.
   - You should ask specific questions to understand if the customer is satisfied and if they have had any problems with the product or service.
   - The seller should handle any concerns with empathy and professionalism, and if appropriate, may request a recommendation or refer other products.

2. **Customer instructions:**
   - The customer must provide answers based on the assigned profile. You can express satisfaction or mention problems you've had.
   - If necessary, the customer can present concerns or suggestions for the salesperson to practice problem solving.

3. **Instructions for the observer (if applicable):**
   - The observer should take notes on the interaction, including the salesperson's empathy, clarity of questions, and how they handle any customer concerns.
   - You should be ready to give constructive feedback on the effectiveness of the call and how the salesperson can improve their post-sales follow-up approach.

Step 3: Performing the after-sales call simulation
1. **Start of the call: Thank you to the customer:**
   - The salesperson starts the call with a friendly greeting and a sincere thank you for the purchase.
   - **Startup example:** "Hello, [Customer Name]. I am [Your Name] from [Company Name]. I wanted to thank you for trusting us and our security system. Could you take a few minutes to tell me what your experience has been like so far?"

2. **Customer satisfaction verification:**
   - The seller should ask about the customer's experience with the product or service. You can ask open-ended questions to invite the customer to share their opinion.
   - **Example question:** "Have you found everything in order with the installation? Is there anything you'd like to share about using the system so far?"

3. **Gathering feedback and resolving concerns**:
    - If the customer expresses any issues or concerns, the salesperson should approach them with empathy, offer an immediate solution, or coordinate the necessary support.
    - **Example of handling trepidation**: "I'm so sorry to hear that you've been struggling with the setup. Let me schedule a technical visit to have one of our experts review you in person."
4. **Request recommendations (optional)**:
    - If the customer expresses satisfaction and is receptive, the salesperson can ask for a recommendation or ask if they know anyone who might be interested in the product or service.
    - **Example of a referral request**: "We are very happy that you are satisfied with our system. If you know someone who is also interested in improving the security of their home, we would be happy to help. In addition, we offer special benefits for each referral."

Step 4: Evaluation and feedback
1. **Feedback between salesperson and customer**:
    - After the call, the customer provides their impression of the interaction, highlighting strengths and suggesting possible areas for improvement for the salesperson.

2. **Observer assessment (if applicable)**:
    - The observer provides a detailed assessment, focusing on aspects such as:
        - **Empathy and kindness**: Did the salesperson show a friendly and empathetic tone?
        - **Clarity in questions**: Were the salesperson's questions clear and direct?
        - **Troubleshooting**: Did the salesperson provide an adequate response to any customer concerns?
        - **Ability to encourage referrals**: Did the salesperson take the opportunity to ask for a recommendation naturally?

3. **Role rotation**:
    - Change roles so that all participants can practice both the salesperson and customer roles.
    - It provides new products and customer profiles for salespeople to experience different types of after-sales situations.

Step 5: Group discussion and final reflection
1. **Group discussion:**
    - After all participants have practiced, gather the group to share experiences and discuss the techniques they felt were most effective.
    - Ask participants what challenges they encountered in handling the call and how they overcame them.

2. **Reflection on after-sales follow-up:**
    - It invites salespeople to reflect on the importance of after-sales follow-up in customer loyalty and satisfaction.
    - Discuss how good follow-up can help build loyalty, get recommendations, and turn the customer into a brand ambassador.

Objective:
This exercise allows salespeople to practice after-sales follow-up in a structured way, with a focus on empathy, problem-solving, and relationship building. By receiving direct feedback, salespeople can identify areas for improvement and develop skills to handle different types of after-sales situations, fostering customer satisfaction and loyalty.

5. Role-playing exercise for consultative selling: Identification of needs and proposal of solution

Consultative **selling** focuses on understanding the customer's specific needs in order to offer a customized solution. In this exercise, participants will practice identifying needs, asking key questions, and tailoring their sales proposition to the customer's particular situation. Through role-playing, salespeople will be able to improve their active listening, analysis, and personalization skills in the sales process.

Instructions:
1. **Define the product or service:** Choose a product or service for the exercise. It can be something complex, such as business management software, that requires a detailed needs analysis.
2. **Assign roles:** One participant will be the salesperson and another the customer, who must have a specific profile with needs and concerns about the product or service.
3. **Needs discovery simulation:** The salesperson should ask open-ended and specific questions to discover the customer's needs and goals.
4. **Solution proposal:** Based on the customer's responses, the salesperson should present a solution proposal tailored to their needs,

highlighting the benefits and how the product or service will help achieve their goals.
5. **Evaluation and feedback**: After the simulation, participants and observers should discuss the effectiveness of the salesperson in identifying needs and adapting the proposal. Strengths and opportunities for improvement must be identified.

Step by step for the role-playing exercise in consultative sales

Step 1: Preparing the Exercise
1. **Pair up and assign roles**:
   - Form pairs of participants, assigning one the role of **salesperson** and the other the role of **customer**.
   - If the group is large, you can designate an **additional observer** to take notes and provide feedback at the end of the simulation.

2. **Select the product or service**:
   - Provide each couple with a product or service that requires consultative analysis, such as business management software or a financial advisory plan.
   - **Product/service example**: An inventory management software for a product distribution company.

3. **Create the customer profile**:
   - Define a profile for the client that includes the context of their business, their objectives, possible needs and concerns.
   - **Customer profile example**: An operations manager at a distribution company who is looking to reduce inventory errors and optimize lead time, but is concerned about implementation costs.

4. **Objective of the exercise**:
   - The salesperson's goal is to discover the customer's specific needs, present them with a customized solution, and get their commitment for a next stage (demo, quote, or trial).

Step 2: Instructions for participants
1. **Instructions for the seller**:
   - The salesperson should start the conversation with open-ended questions to understand the context and the customer's needs.

- You must listen carefully, identify opportunities, and tailor your proposal to the problems and objectives mentioned by the client.
- It is important for the salesperson to show empathy and position themselves as an advisor who seeks to help the customer, rather than just selling them a product.

2. **Customer instructions**:
   - The customer must respond realistically, based on the profile provided. You can express your needs, as well as any concerns or limitations.
   - You should provide details about your business challenges and how you expect the solution to solve them.
   - The customer may raise objections or doubts for the salesperson to practice how to handle consultative selling.

3. **Instructions for the observer (if applicable)**:
   - The observer should take notes on the salesperson's performance, including their ability to ask relevant questions, identify the customer's needs, and tailor the proposal.
   - You should assess the vendor's clarity and effectiveness in presenting the solution, as well as their ability to demonstrate empathy and understanding.

Step 3: Conducting consultative selling role-playing

1. **Conversation starter: Open-ended questions and discovery of needs**:
   - The salesperson starts with a greeting and open-ended questions to get general information about the customer's business and their goals.
   - **Sample questions**:
     - "Tell me a little bit about your company. What are your main challenges in inventory management?"
     - "What would you like to improve in your current processes?"

2. **Deepening of the client's needs**:
   - As the customer responds, the salesperson should ask additional questions to dig deeper into specific needs and concerns.
   - **Example of additional questions**:
     - "What is the impact of inventory errors on your daily operation?"

- "What kind of system has it used so far, and what has it lacked?"

3. **Presentation of a personalized proposal for a solution:**
   - Based on the information obtained, the salesperson should present an adapted solution, explaining how the product or service can solve the customer's specific problems.
   - **Example presentation:**
     - "Our inventory management software automates stock updates in real-time, reducing errors and optimizing visibility into your products. In addition, we offer ongoing support to ensure that the implementation is as non-disruptive as possible."

4. **Response to customer questions and objections:**
   - The customer can ask questions about the proposal or raise objections, and the salesperson must respond clearly and confidently.
   - **Example of objection:**
     - Customer: "I'm worried about the cost of implementing a new system."
     - Salesperson: "I understand, the initial investment can be a concern. However, we have seen our customers recoup the cost through reduced errors and efficiency improvements. We can discuss financing options if you are interested."

5. **Consultative closure: Next step proposal:**
   - After addressing the doubts, the salesperson suggests a concrete next step (a demo, follow-up meeting, or budget proposal).
   - **Closing example:**
     - "I'd love to show you a personalized demo of the system so you can see how it can fit your business. How about we schedule one for next week?"

Step 4: Evaluation and feedback
1. **Exchange of impressions between seller and customer:**
   - After the simulation is complete, the client shares their impression of the interaction, highlighting the strengths and suggesting aspects that could have been handled differently.

2. **Observer assessment (if applicable):**
   - The observer provides feedback on key aspects such as:

- **Quality of questions**: Were the salesperson's questions effective in identifying the customer's needs?
- **Adaptation of the proposal**: Was the proposed solution adapted to the client's problems and objectives?
- **Empathy and professionalism**: Did the salesperson show empathy and an advisory attitude, rather than just selling?

3. **Role rotation**:
   - Change roles so that all participants can practice both the salesperson and customer roles.
   - Assign new products or services and customer profiles for sellers to experiment with different consultative selling scenarios.

Step 5: Group discussion and final reflection

1. **Group discussion**:
   - After everyone has participated, gather the group to discuss the techniques they felt were most effective and the challenges they encountered.
   - Ask participants how they adapted their questions and proposals based on the client's needs.

2. **Reflection on consultative selling**:
   - It invites salespeople to reflect on the importance of listening to the customer and offering solutions adapted to their needs.
   - Discuss how a consultative approach contributes to building trusting relationships and fostering long-term customer loyalty.

Objective:

This role-playing exercise allows salespeople to practice consultative selling in a controlled environment, where they can experience the importance of active listening and personalization of the value proposition. By receiving direct feedback, participants identify areas for improvement and strengthen their abilities to understand and respond to customer needs, thus increasing their chances of success in real sales situations.

6. Performance evaluation exercise: Measurement of sales objectives and KPIs

This exercise allows salespeople to reflect on their performance based on sales **goals** and **KPIs**. By assessing their progress, participants can identify areas for improvement and establish concrete action plans to achieve their goals. This exercise encourages self-management and continuous development, helping salespeople focus on the key aspects that drive their success.

Instructions:
1. **Define KPIs and goals**: Provide salespeople with a list of key KPIs, such as the number of closed sales, conversion rate, and customer satisfaction, along with specific goals.
2. **Self-assessment**: Each salesperson should analyze their recent performance and compare it to the established objectives. You should write down your accomplishments and areas for improvement.
3. **Group evaluation**: Form small groups where each salesperson shares their results and discusses strategies that have helped them achieve their goals or challenges they have faced.
4. **Develop an improvement plan**: Based on group feedback and self-assessment, each salesperson should develop a personal improvement plan that includes specific actions to improve their KPIs.

Step-by-step for the sales performance evaluation exercise

Step 1: Preparing the exercise
1. **Define KPIs and sales objectives:**
   - Before starting the exercise, provide a list of **key KPIs** that will be used to evaluate performance. These may include:
     - **Number of closed sales**: Total sales made in a period.
     - **Conversion rate**: Percentage of prospects who converted into customers.
     - **Average Sale Value**: Average value of each closed sale.
     - **Customer satisfaction**: The level of customer satisfaction measured by surveys or scores.
     - **Number of referrals earned**: The number of referred customers generated from existing customers.

2. **Set sales goals:**
   - Provide sellers with specific goals for each KPI. These may vary depending on the roles and experience of each participant.
   - **Examples of objectives:**
     - Reach 10 closed sales in the last quarter.
     - Maintain a conversion rate of 30%.
     - Achieve an average sales value of $500.
     - Obtain a customer satisfaction score of 4.5 or higher.

3. **Prepare self-assessment tools:**
   - Distribute self-assessment forms or templates where salespeople can record their performance against each KPI and objective.
   - Be sure to include space for comments and reflections on what they considered to be their strengths and areas for improvement.

Step 2: Instructions for participants

1. **Conduct a self-assessment:**
   - Each participant must complete the self-assessment form, indicating their results in relation to each KPI and comparing them with the established objectives.
   - Salespeople should write down accomplishments and reflect on any gaps between their performance and goals.

2. **Identify strengths and areas for improvement:**
   - Ask participants to identify their **strengths**, such as techniques that helped them close sales, strategies to improve customer satisfaction, or effective practices for obtaining referrals.
   - They should also point out **areas for improvement**, such as aspects of the conversion rate that could be optimized or methods to increase the average value of sales.

3. **Establish a personal improvement plan:**
   - Ask salespeople to develop a **self-improvement plan** based on their evaluation. This plan should include specific, measurable actions to meet or exceed your sales goals in the next period.
   - **Example of an improvement plan:**
     - **Goal:** Increase the conversion rate to 35% in the next quarter.

- **Action**: Participate in an objection handling course to improve the ability to close sales.
- **Measure of success**: Increase in conversion rate in the next performance report.

Step 3: Small group assessment
1. **Form discussion groups**:
   - Group participants into teams of 3 or 4 people. Each one must share their results and their personal improvement plan with the group.

2. **Share strategies and tips**:
   - Participants should exchange strategies that have worked for them and provide advice on how to overcome the challenges they have faced.
   - Encourage them to share concrete examples of actions that helped them improve their KPIs, such as effective closing techniques or strategies to increase customer satisfaction.

3. **Constructive feedback**:
   - Each member of the group should provide constructive feedback on each other's improvement plans. Feedback should be specific, highlighting what they find positive and offering suggestions for improvement.

Step 4: Reflection and general discussion
1. **Gather the whole group for a general discussion**:
   - Ask each group to share the most prominent strategies and common challenges they identified during the evaluation.
   - It discusses best practices for improving each KPI and allows salespeople to ask questions or provide additional suggestions.

2. **Reflection on performance**:
   - It invites participants to reflect on the importance of measuring their performance regularly and adjusting their sales strategies based on the results obtained.
   - Highlights the importance of self-assessment and the establishment of improvement plans, as well as the usefulness of feedback from peers.

Step 5: Follow-up and review of the improvement plan
1. **Establish a follow-up plan:**
   - Invite salespeople to review their self-improvement plan within a certain period, such as in the next quarter. This will allow them to evaluate whether the actions they have implemented are generating the expected results.

2. **Schedule a progress review:**
   - Schedule a follow-up meeting where sellers can discuss their progress and receive additional support. This encourages accountability and continuity in developing their skills.

Exercise objective

This exercise allows salespeople to reflect in a structured way on their sales performance, identify areas for improvement, and establish a concrete action plan to achieve their goals. By sharing their experiences and receiving feedback from their peers, participants can develop a clearer and more proactive approach towards self-managing their performance and professional growth.

Bonus: How to define sales KPIs

Defining sales KPIs is essential to measure success and evaluate the performance of the sales team. These indicators allow salespeople and managers to monitor progress toward goals, identify areas for improvement, and make informed decisions. Here's a simple process for defining sales KPIs effectively.

Step 1: Identify your overall sales goals
1. **Determine the company's objectives:**
   - Before setting KPIs, define sales targets in line with the company's overall goals. This can include increasing revenue, attracting new customers, or increasing retention of existing customers.
   - **Example goal:** "Increase sales revenue by 20% in the next year."

2. **Define specific sales goals:**
   - Translate overall objectives into specific, achievable goals for the sales team that can be quantified.
   - **Example of a specific goal:** "Achieve 100 new sales of annual subscriptions to the service in the first quarter."

Step 2: Select the sales KPIs that support the objectives

1. **Identify indicators that measure progress:**
   - Choose KPIs that measure progress toward set goals. They should be measurable and reflect key areas of performance.
   - **Examples of KPIs:**
     - **Number of new sales:** Measures the number of sales closed in a period.
     - **Conversion rate:** Measures the percentage of prospects who convert into customers.
     - **Average Sale Value:** Calculate the average value of each transaction.
     - **Sales cycle length:** Measures the average time it takes to close a sale from first contact to closing.

2. **Ensure that KPIs are specific and relevant:**
   - Each KPI should be directly related to achieving the overall goal and be relevant to the sales team.
   - **Example:** If the goal is to increase the number of new customers, the KPIs of "Number of New Sales" and "Conversion Rate" will be particularly relevant.

Step 3: Set quantifiable goals for each KPI

1. **Assign numerical values to KPIs:**
   - Define specific goals for each KPI, allowing you to evaluate the sales team's performance clearly and objectively.
   - **Example of Goals:**
     - Number of New Sales: Reach 25 new sales per month.
     - Conversion Rate: Maintain a conversion rate of at least 30%.
     - Average Sale Value: Achieve an average of $800 per transaction.

2. **Define a measurement period:**
   - Determine the time period over which you will measure each KPI (monthly, quarterly, yearly).
   - **Example:** Evaluate the "Number of New Sales" and "Conversion Rate" on a monthly basis to review progress and adjust strategies as needed.

Step 4: Ensure regular measurement and monitoring of KPIs

1. **Establish a system to monitor progress:**
   - Use CRM tools or spreadsheets to record and monitor KPI results on a regular basis.

- **Example**: Implement a dashboard that shows the daily or weekly progress of each KPI for the sales team.

2. **Review and adjust KPIs as needed**:
    - Conduct periodic evaluations of KPIs to verify if goals are being achieved. Adjust KPIs if targets change or if current indicators are not serving their purpose.
    - **Example**: If the "Conversion Rate" goal is not being reached, research the reasons and adjust sales tactics to improve it.

Step 5: Communicate and align KPIs with the sales team
1. **Share KPIs and goals with the team**:
    - Make sure the entire sales team understands KPIs and their importance to achieving overall goals.
    - **Example**: Organize a meeting to explain the KPIs, their goals, and how each salesperson can contribute to achieving them.

2. **Encourage responsibility and commitment**:
    - It promotes a sense of responsibility and ownership among team members, encouraging their commitment to achieve KPIs.
    - **Example**: Assign specific responsibilities to each salesperson and regularly track their progress against KPIs.

Conclusion

Defining effective sales KPIs involves aligning them with the company's objectives, choosing relevant indicators, setting clear goals, monitoring progress, and communicating the process to the team. By following these steps, companies can evaluate the sales team's performance, identify opportunities for improvement, and ensure that everyone is working toward common, measurable goals.

Chapter 19

Case Studies

Next, I will take you by the hand with 3 practical cases using strategies that help you establish a good interaction with potential customers in real sales situations, dealing with a tangible, intangible, and combined product.

19.1 Case study:

Sale of tangibles - Home appliances

In this case study, we'll work through the sales process for a **tangible appliance**: a high-end refrigerator. The goal is to guide the customer from the first contact to the closing of the sale, using sales techniques and addressing any objections that may arise. This exercise will also include hands-on activities at each step so that you can apply the techniques discussed in real-time.

Context of the case

Product: High-end refrigerator with food preservation technology, adjustable temperature control, and energy-efficient design.
Customer: A family of four looking to upgrade their current refrigerator to a more modern and efficient one.
Scenario: The sale takes place at an appliance store where the customer has shown interest in the product and wants to receive more information before making a decision.

1. First contact: Greeting and discovery of needs
The first contact is essential to establish a relationship of trust with the customer. Here, the goal is to understand the customer's needs, using an initial open conversation.

Action: Greeting and introducing yourself
- **Salesperson**: "Hello, welcome to [Store Name]. My name is [Your Name], and I will be happy to help you. I see that they are interested in our refrigerators. Specifically what are they looking for in a new refrigerator?"

Practical activity:
1. **Active listening**: Make sure to practice **active listening** as the customer describes their needs. Take mental notes on the keywords they use.
2. **Discovery question**: Ask them an open-ended question that allows you to better understand what they value in a refrigerator, such as:
    - "What features do you consider most important in a refrigerator?"

Exercise:
- **Reflect** on a hypothetical response from the customer and write down what features they would value. Example: "We are interested in energy efficiency and storage space."

2. Product presentation: Adaptation to customer needs
Once you've figured out the customer's needs, it's time to present the product in a way that highlights how it meets those needs. Tailor your presentation to what the client has expressed.

Action: Focus on benefits
- **Seller:** "This refrigerator is perfect if you're looking for energy efficiency and a large space. It has an A++ energy rating, which will allow you to save on your electricity bill. In addition, it has a capacity of 500 liters, enough to store fresh food for the whole family."

Practical activity:
1. **Presentation adjustment:** Select two product features and tailor the presentation to highlight how they align with what the customer values.
2. **Demonstration in action:** Physically points out the refrigerator's features, showing how the temperature control and internal space work. This allows the customer to visualize how the product meets their expectations.

Exercise:
- **Write a short 3-4 line presentation** highlighting the benefits of the product based on what the customer valued (e.g., energy efficiency and space).

---

3. Handling objections: Responding effectively
It is common for the client to express some doubt or objection before making the decision. Handling objections is crucial to clearing their concerns and maintaining interest.

Action: Respond to objections
Suppose the customer expresses an objection about the price:
- **Customer:** "This refrigerator is more expensive than other models we've seen."
- **Salesperson:** "I understand, [Customer's Name]. This model has a higher price tag, but it is designed to save energy, which will allow them to reduce costs in the long run. In addition, it comes with an extended five-year warranty. Would you like to know more about financing options?"

Practical activity:
1. **Identify and validate the objection**: Listen to the objection and respond with empathy before presenting a solution.
2. **Propose an alternative or solution**: Offer options that mitigate objection, such as financing or discounts, if available.

Exercise:
- **Think of a common objection** (e.g., "How trustworthy is this brand?") and **write a response** that validates and addresses it using the social evidence technique. Example: "Many customers were hesitant about the brand at first, but have told us that they are delighted with the durability of the product after several years of use. Would you like to hear some testimonies?"

4. Closing proposal: Choosing the right closing technique
The closing is the step where the customer confirms their purchase decision. Here, the salesperson should use a closing technique that fits the situation and the customer's level of interest.

Action: Apply the incentive closure
If the customer shows interest, but is still hesitant, you can offer an incentive.
- **Salesperson:** "Today we are offering a 10% discount on this model and also free delivery. Would you like to take advantage of this offer and secure the refrigerator now?"

Practical activity:
1. **Select the closing technique**: Choose the most appropriate closing technique according to the client's interest. If the customer seems undecided between two models, use the alternative closure.
2. **Highlight the offer**: Show the customer how the incentive adds additional value to their purchase and generates urgency to make a decision.

Exercise:
- **Write a short script** using the alternate closure in case the customer hesitates between two refrigerators. Example: "We can opt for this model, which is more affordable, or we can choose the premium model that includes a high-capacity freezer. Which of these best fits your needs?"

5. Thank you and confirmation: Reinforce the customer's decision
After the customer confirms the purchase, it's important to thank them and reassure them that they've made an excellent decision. This not only

closes the sale, but also establishes a relationship of trust for future interactions.

Action: Appreciation and reinforcement of the decision

- **Salesperson:** "Thank you for your purchase! They have made an excellent choice. This refrigerator will not only allow them to save on energy, but it will also last for many years. If you have any questions, please do not hesitate to contact us. We will be here to help them."

Practical activity:

1. **Express gratitude:** Use positive language that reinforces customer satisfaction with their purchase.
2. **Provide tracking information:** If the store offers after-sales support, make sure the customer has all the necessary information.

Exercise:

- **Write a thank you message** that reinforces the benefits of the product and offers additional support. Example: "Thank you for choosing our refrigerator. With its high energy efficiency, we are sure it will be an excellent addition to your home. Please feel free to contact us if you have any questions; We're here to help."

Conclusion

In this case study, we've covered the entire process of selling a refrigerator, from first contact to closing and thank you. Through these activities and exercises, you've practiced key skills such as active listening, handling objections, and applying closure techniques. Not only do these techniques help you close the sale, but they also foster a positive customer experience, building trust and laying the foundation for a long-term relationship.

19.2 Case study:

Sale of intangibles - Life insurance

In this case study, you will work on the sales process for an **intangible product:** life insurance. The goal is to guide the customer from the first contact to the closing of the sale, using sales techniques and addressing any objections that may arise. This exercise will also include hands-on activities at each step so that you can apply sales techniques specific to intangibles, where the benefits are not immediately visible or tangible.

Context of the case

Product: Life insurance that includes additional benefits such as coverage for serious illnesses, long-term savings and financial advice.
Client: A 35-year-old professional, married with two young children, who is evaluating options to protect his family and plan financially.
Scenario: The sale is made through a meeting scheduled at the client's office, where they have shown interest in learning about life insurance options and additional benefits.

1. First contact: Establish relationships and discover needs

In the sale of intangibles, establishing a relationship of trust is essential. Here, the goal is to discover the customer's needs and understand their motivations, using an open conversation focused on their priorities.

Action: Greet and ask exploratory questions

- **Salesperson**: "Hello, [Customer's Name]. Thank you for taking the time to meet today. My name is [Your Name], and I will be happy to help you explore life insurance options. To begin with, could you tell me a little bit more about what you are concerned about and what you seek to protect?"

Practical activity:

1. **Active listening**: Practice **active listening**, picking up not only on what the customer says, but how they say it. Pay attention to their priorities and concerns.
2. **Discovery questions**: Ask open-ended questions that allow you to understand what aspects are most important to the customer, such as:
    - "What aspects do you consider a priority to protect your family?"
    - "Have you thought about how you'd like life insurance to support your long-term financial goals?"

Exercise:

- **Write a list of three questions** that could help uncover the customer's life insurance needs. Example: "What are your main concerns in terms of financial security for your family?"

2. Product presentation: Focus on personal and emotional benefits

With an intangible like life insurance, it's critical to present the product in a way that resonates with the client's values and goals, showing how the insurance will bring you security and peace of mind.

Action: Tailor the presentation to the client's needs
- **Salesperson:** "Based on what you've told me, it seems that protecting your family's well-being is your top priority. This life insurance offers comprehensive coverage to ensure that no matter what, your family is protected and financially supported. Plus, it includes a long-term savings plan that could help you plan for your children's future."

Practical activity:
1. **Emphasize emotional benefits:** In the presentation, highlight the emotional benefits, such as the peace of mind and security that insurance provides.
2. **Demonstrate how the product meets needs:** Explains how specific insurance meets the customer's financial and protection goals, linking product features to what the customer valued.

Exercise:
- **Write a brief description** of the product that includes an emotional benefit and a functional benefit. Example: "This insurance not only gives you peace of mind knowing that your family will be protected, but it also allows you to build savings that can be used to fund your children's college education."

3. Handling objections: Addressing doubts and responding to concerns

In intangible sales, objections are usually related to the lack of tangibility and the perception of cost versus value. It's critical to address these concerns with empathy and demonstrate the value of life insurance.

Action: Listen to and validate the objection
When the client has an objection about the cost of insurance:
- **Client:** "That seems like a high investment for something I'm not sure if we're going to need."
- **Salesperson:** "I understand that it may seem like a considerable investment, [Customer's Name]. The reason why our customers opt for this insurance is because it provides them with support in difficult times. And, at the same time, it has the potential to create a savings fund that you can use later. Would you like to know how this insurance can be an investment in your future?"

Practical activity:
1. **Identify the main objection:** Listen to the customer's objection and define what their main concern is.
2. **Respond with empathy and provide information:** Validate the customer's concern and offer a response that allows them to understand the value and benefits of insurance.

Exercise:
- **Write a response to the common objection** of "I don't need life insurance yet" using the positive reframing technique. Example: "I get your point. We often think that insurance is only necessary in emergency situations, but many find that by obtaining it earlier, they ensure better conditions and rates that benefit in the long term. Would you like to know how this coverage can be tailored to your current and future needs?"

4. Closure proposal: Select the appropriate closure technique for intangibles

To close the sale of an intangible, it is important that the customer feels confident in their decision and that they perceive the value of the protection that the insurance offers them. Closing benefits or trial are effective options in this case.

Action: Use profit closing
- **Salesperson**: "With this insurance, you not only get coverage to protect your family, but you can also build a savings fund that will serve you well in the future. What do you think if we proceed to ensure this protection from today?"

Practical activity:
1. **Highlight long-term benefits**: Show the customer how life insurance provides value over time and not just in the present.
2. **Invite the customer to take action**: Use a call to action that reinforces the safety and security that insurance will provide.

Exercise:
- **Write a closing proposal** using the test closure, if the client needs more time to decide. Example: "I understand that you would like to consider it more. How about offering a free counseling trial to explore how this insurance can benefit your family? If you decide to move forward, we can formalize it."

5. Thank you and confirmation: Strengthen the customer's decision

At the end of the sales process, it is important to thank the customer and reinforce the importance of their decision. This helps build trust and open the door for future services or referrals.

Action: Appreciation and follow-up
- **Salesperson**: "Thank you for trusting us, [Customer's Name]. I am confident that this insurance will provide you and your family with the security you need. We will keep in touch to make sure everything is

running smoothly. If at any time you have questions, please don't hesitate to call me."

Practical activity:
1. **Express genuine appreciation**: Use words of appreciation that show your appreciation for the trust the customer has placed in you.
2. **Offer future support**: Explain how the customer can contact you for support or clarification throughout the term of the insurance.

Exercise:
- **Write a closing message** that reaffirms the customer's decision and offers additional support. Example: "Thank you for allowing us to be part of your protection plan. I am confident that this insurance will give you and your family peace of mind. Remember that I am here for any questions or queries. Have a great day!"

Conclusion

In this case study, we have addressed the process of selling an intangible, from the first contact to the closing and the final thank you. Through these activities and exercises, you have practiced fundamental techniques for selling intangible products, which require a special focus on building trust and communicating emotional value. By applying these principles, you'll be able to improve your sales skills and build stronger, longer-lasting relationships with your customers, ensuring they feel protected and supported at all times.

19.3 Case study:

Combined sale of tangibles and intangibles - Home security system with monitoring plan

In this case study, we'll explore how to sell a **tangible product** (a security camera system) and an associated **intangible service** (a monthly monitoring plan). Storytelling will be used as the main tool to connect with the customer, address objections and highlight the value of both the tangible and intangible product.

Context of the case

Tangible product: Home security camera system, with motion detection, HD recording and night vision functions.
Intangible product: 24/7 monitoring service with real-time alerts and direct connection with authorities.

Client: A young couple who have recently moved into a home in a new neighborhood and are concerned about the safety of their home.
Scenario: The sale takes place in a store specializing in security systems, where customers are looking for options to protect their home.

1. First contact: Establish connection and discover needs using storytelling

In this first step, the goal is to connect with the customer and discover their needs. Using a story helps illustrate how the security system has helped other customers in similar situations.

Action: Greeting and using a welcome story
- **Salesperson**: "Hello, welcome to [Store Name]. My name is [Your Name]. Just a few weeks ago I helped a couple who, like you, had recently moved and were looking for a security solution for their new home. They wanted to be reassured knowing that they were protected at all times. What are you most concerned about about the safety of your home?"

Practical activity:
1. **Active listening**: Pay attention to customers' responses and mentally write down the concerns they express.
2. **Story building**: Think of a story that you can use to connect with the customer's needs, that resonates with their current situation, and that shows how your product and service have helped others.

Exercise:
- **Write a short story** that you can use to break the ice with a client who is concerned about the safety of their home. Example: "I remember a family that had just moved and was not used to having a security system. After installing the system, they told me how calm they felt knowing that their home was protected even when they were away."

2. Product presentation: Show the value of the tangible through a relevant story

It is important to present the camera system by highlighting its features and benefits, but also integrating a story that allows customers to visualize themselves using the product in their daily lives.

Action: Describe the system and tell a story about its use
- **Seller**: "This security camera system has motion detection and night vision, perfect for protecting all areas of the house. We recently installed this same system at the home of a client who travels a lot for

work. He told me that one night he received an alert while he was away and could see from his cell phone that everything was in order. He felt really reassured knowing that he could be aware of his home in real time."

Practical activity:
1. **Highlight relevant features**: Based on the concerns customers have mentioned, choose two or three key features of the camera system that offer peace of mind.
2. **Story building**: Use a concrete example that illustrates how those features have been useful to other customers.

Exercise:
- **Write a short story** that uses a feature of the system (such as night vision) to highlight how that feature has been useful to other customers. Example: "One of our clients received an alert while she was sleeping and, thanks to night vision, she could see that an animal had approached the yard. The camera captured everything clearly, and she felt safe to see what was happening without leaving the house."

3. Service presentation: Showing the value of the intangible using storytelling

With the monitoring service, the objective is to explain how the peace of mind it offers goes beyond the simple tangible product, highlighting the importance of having a backup in emergency situations.

Action: Explain the monitoring service with a security story
- **Salesperson:** "In addition to the camera system, we offer a monitoring service that guarantees that, in the event of any emergency situation, they will receive an alert and will be able to communicate directly with the authorities. Recently, a client who lives alone had an overnight medical emergency. Thanks to the connection to monitoring, we were able to send help quickly. He was so grateful to have someone vouch for him when he needed it most."

Practical activity:
1. **Emphasize the value of monitoring**: Explain how the monitoring service brings an additional level of security that the product alone cannot offer.
2. **Incorporate a value story**: Use an example that demonstrates the importance of having real-time support and how this service has made a difference for others.

Exercise:
- **Write a story** that highlights how the monitoring service has helped a customer in an emergency situation. Example: "A customer traveling for work received a notification on his cell phone about activity at home. Although he was not at home, the monitoring service was in charge of reviewing the situation and notifying the authorities, guaranteeing that everything was under control. The customer felt really safe knowing that they had a backup."

4. Handling objections: Addressing doubts using stories and testimonials

It is common for customers to have doubts or feel insecure about investing in an intangible product such as monitoring. Here, the stories help illustrate how others overcame similar doubts and felt satisfied with the decision.

Action: Respond with a story that addresses the objection

Let's say the customer has questions about the monthly cost of the monitoring service:
- **Client:** "I'm not sure I want to pay a monthly fee for monitoring."
- **Salesperson:** "I understand, [Customer's Name]. A recent customer also thought the same thing at first, but told us that after an incident in his neighborhood, he felt more at ease having this support. Sometimes, knowing that you are protected and that you have someone who will help you when you need it, is worth much more than what the monthly fee costs."

Practical activity:
1. **Identify and validate the objection:** Listen to the customer's objection and use a story to address the concern in an empathetic way.
2. **Show testimonials:** Accompany the story with a testimonial from a customer who has had a positive experience with the service.

Exercise:
- **Write a short story** to answer the objection about the monthly cost. Example: "One of our customers shared that he was hesitant about the cost at first, but after seeing how quickly the service responded when there was an attempted intrusion on his street, he has no regrets. Now he feels safe, knowing that there is always someone on the lookout."

5. Closing proposal: Use storytelling to reaffirm the client's decision

For closing, storytelling can be used for the customer to visualize how the product and service together will provide the security and peace of mind they are looking for. Both alternative and benefit closures can be used.

Action: Apply benefit closing with an ending story
- **Salesperson:** "By combining the camera system with the monitoring service, you'll not only be protecting your home, but you're also buying peace of mind. I remember a family who was hesitant at first, but after the installation, they felt so calm that they decided to add the monitoring service to their parents' house as well. They knew they would be protected at all times. Would you like to secure this protection today?"

Practical activity:
1. **Summarize combined value:** Explain how both the tangible product and the intangible service complement each other and provide long-term value.
2. **Invite the customer to visualize the benefits:** Use a closure that allows the customer to imagine how the product and service will improve their life.

Exercise:
- Write a closing proposal that includes a summary of the value and a call to action. Example: "With this camera system and monitoring, they will be covered at all times. One of our clients told us that, since he installed it, his family has slept peacefully, knowing that they are protected. What do you think if we proceed with the installation so that you can enjoy this same peace of mind?"

6. Appreciation and follow-up: Strengthen the relationship with an inspiring story

After closing the sale, it is important to thank the customer and reassure them that they have made a wise decision. An inspiring story helps reaffirm that they have made the best choice for their safety.

Action: Final thank-you using a story of tranquility
- **Salesperson:** "Thank you for trusting us, [Customer's Name]. Recently, a client told us that since she has the system, she feels much more at ease about leaving her children at home, even when she is not there. I am sure that this system will give you the same peace of mind. If you have any questions or need help, we will be here for you."

Practical activity:
1. **Express gratitude and reinforce the decision:** Sincerely thank the customer for their trust and use a story that highlights the emotional benefits of the product and service.
2. **Offer support and follow-up:** Provide them with information so they feel supported anytime they need it.

Exercise:
- **Write a closing message** that reinforces the customer's decision and offers reassurance. Example: "Thank you for choosing us to protect your home. We know this investment will give you a lot of peace of mind, and we'll be here to make sure you receive the best service. Have a great day!"

Conclusion

In this case study, we have addressed the use of storytelling in the process of selling tangible and intangible products, from the first contact to the closing and the final thanks. Stories not only help connect emotionally with the customer, but they also allow you to overcome objections and highlight the value of the product and service. By practicing these techniques, you can create a memorable and effective sales experience, building stronger, longer-lasting relationships with your customers.

Final summary

Comprehensive sales strategies, after-sales, and customer loyalty

The successful sales process does not end with the initial transaction, but continues through a solid **after-sales** and **loyalty** strategy. This summary synthesizes the key points addressed in the previous chapters, covering everything from sales techniques and objection handling to the importance of after-sales customer service and attention. Through these elements, a comprehensive experience is built that not only ensures customer satisfaction, but also promotes loyalty, sustainable growth, and long-term success for the company.

1. Sales strategies and closing techniques

The sales process begins with the initial contact and continues until the **closing** of the transaction, using techniques that allow the customer's interest to be transformed into a purchase commitment. Featured techniques include:

- **Direct assumption closing**: Acting as if the customer has already decided to buy, guiding the conversation to the next steps.
- **Closing the alternative**: Offer the customer two options, focusing the decision on the **how** and not on the **yes**.
- **Closing benefits**: Highlight the key benefits of the product or service to persuade the customer to take action.
- **Incentive Closure**: Offer an additional benefit, such as a discount or free service, to incentivize immediate closure.

These techniques help address customer concerns and facilitate a natural transition towards closing the sale, ensuring that the experience is positive and satisfying.

2. After-sales as a pillar of loyalty and long-term value

After-sales is essential to maintain the relationship with the customer and ensure their long-term satisfaction. Through after-sales, the company can provide continuous support, solve problems, and strengthen customer trust. Among the essential elements of after-sales are:

- **Customer service**: Providing accessible, efficient, and personalized service that caters to customer needs after purchase.
- **Proactive follow-up**: Follow up after the sale to ensure the customer is satisfied and to detect any issues that may arise.
- **Feedback and continuous improvement**: Collect and analyze customer feedback to identify areas for improvement and adjust sales and after-sales strategies on an ongoing basis.

A quality after-sales not only strengthens the relationship with the customer, but also increases the chances of additional sales and recommendations, turning satisfied customers into brand ambassadors.

3. Customer service in the after-sales service as a competitive advantage

Customer **service** during after-sales is a key differentiator in a competitive market. Offering a quality service involves several components:

- **Empathy and active listening**: Understanding the customer's concerns and emotions to provide solutions that truly meet their needs.
- **Efficiency and quick problem resolution**: Address and resolve any issues quickly, to ensure that the customer maintains a positive experience.
- **Clear and transparent communication**: Inform the customer accurately and honestly about the processes, deadlines and solutions available.
- **Proactivity in follow-up**: Make proactive follow-up contacts to ensure that the customer is satisfied and feels valued.

Offering exceptional after-sales service not only ensures customer satisfaction, but also contributes to **loyalty** and increases the likelihood of future purchases and recommendations.

4. Handling objections and converting into upsells

Objections are a natural part of the sales process and should be seen as opportunities to strengthen the value proposition. Some techniques for handling objections include:

- **Positive reframing**: Changing the customer's perspective on their objection, showing how it can actually be a benefit.
- **Use of storytelling**: Tell stories of other customers who overcame similar doubts and achieved successful results, to connect emotionally with the customer.
- **Presentation of evidence and data**: Provide tangible evidence and data that support the benefits of the product or service, strengthening customer credibility and trust.

By addressing objections constructively and using techniques that reinforce value, the salesperson can overcome the customer's doubts and move toward closing, generating a positive and memorable experience.

5. Getting referral recommendations and sales

The after-sales also opens the door to recommendations and **referral sales**. Satisfied customers are more likely to recommend the company to family, friends, or colleagues. Strategies to facilitate recommendations include:

- **Ask for testimonials**: Ask satisfied customers to share their experience on social media, websites, or through surveys.
- **Offer referral incentives**: Implement a referral program that encourages customers to recommend the company to others by offering exclusive discounts or benefits.
- **Appreciation and Relationship Cultivation**: Sincerely thanking the customer for their purchase and maintaining regular contact to strengthen the long-term relationship.

Encouraging referrals not only expands the customer base, but also strengthens the company's reputation and visibility, increasing its competitiveness and growth.

6. The importance of measuring and continuously improving after-sales service

Measuring **after-sales service** is essential to ensure that the strategies in place are working and that customers are satisfied. Some of the key metrics include:

- **Customer satisfaction (CSAT):** Assesses how satisfied the customer is with the service received.
- **Response and resolution time:** Measures how quickly requests are responded to and issues are resolved.
- **Net Promoter Score (NPS):** Measures how likely the customer is to recommend the company to others, which is an indicator of loyalty.

Continuous improvement based on customer feedback allows the company to adjust and evolve to meet market expectations, which strengthens its value proposition and ensures its long-term relevance.

Sales, after-sales and loyalty are interdependent elements that must be managed in an integral way to maximize the success of any company. From effective sales techniques to satisfaction-oriented after-sales and exceptional customer service, every aspect contributes to building a strong and lasting customer relationship. By adopting these strategies, companies not only manage to satisfy their customers, but also generate loyalty, recommendations, and sustainable growth that allows them to stand out in a competitive market. Customer care and commitment at every stage of the sales process are the key to transforming a transaction into a valuable and long-lasting relationship.

Epilogue

The constant evolution of the world of sales and the path to success

The world of sales is, and always has been, a field of constant change. Over the decades, the industry has seen how the sales approach has evolved from rigid, product-centric techniques to more consultative approaches, focused on building relationships, and tailored to specific customer needs. This process of transformation does not stop; In fact, the speed of change has increased thanks to new technologies, access to information, and changing consumer expectations.

In this context of constant evolution, successful salespeople are those who have learned to **adapt**, to **continuously improve** and to **accept change** as an opportunity to grow. The path to success in sales is not based on achieving a fixed level of skills, but on a commitment to constant learning and the ability to reinvent yourself.

Adaptation as the key to success

In an environment where customers are increasingly informed, demanding, and aware of their options, the ability to adapt to their needs and adjust the sales approach is essential. Adaptation involves being attentive to market trends, new technologies and changes in consumer behavior. This ability allows salespeople to connect with customers in a meaningful way and deliver value to them in a way that feels authentic and relevant.

Technological and digital adaptation

Technology has transformed the world of sales, from CRM tools and data analytics to social media-based sales strategies and digital channels. Salespeople who adopt these tools can gain accurate customer insights, streamline their sales process, and improve efficiency. Technology adaptation also opens up opportunities to connect with customers on new platforms and personalize the shopping experience in ways previously unimaginable.

Adaptation to customer expectations

The ability to listen and respond to changing customer needs is another facet of adaptation. Today, consumers value transparency, authenticity and commitment to values that go beyond the simple transaction. Salespeople who succeed in building relationships based on trust and who genuinely care about the customer's interests are better positioned to succeed in this environment. This means taking a more consultative and personalized approach to sales, and putting the customer at the center of every decision.

Continuous improvement: A lifelong learning cycle

The world of sales demands continuous improvement, both in skill development and in knowledge of products and trends. Successful salespeople are those who don't settle for what they already know, but are constantly looking for ways to improve and expand their capabilities.

Training and personal development

Training isn't just for novice salespeople; it is a fundamental practice for everyone. Salespeople should invest in their personal development through courses, seminars, readings, and the constant practice of new techniques. In addition, sales is a career in which knowledge of products and services is constantly evolving, so being up to date is key to transmitting confidence and credibility.

Self-assessment and feedback

Continuous improvement also involves evaluating one's own performance and seeking feedback. Salespeople who practice self-assessment can identify their strengths and areas for improvement, allowing them to adjust their strategies and move toward success. Feedback from colleagues, supervisors, and even customers can provide valuable insights to refine the sales approach and better adapt to market expectations.

Building a growth mindset to overcome obstacles

The world of sales is challenging, and those who pursue success must be prepared to face obstacles and rejections. This is where a **growth mindset** becomes an invaluable resource. This mindset involves seeing challenges as opportunities to learn and not as failures.

Resilience and persistence

Rejection is a natural part of the sales process. Resilient salespeople understand that every "no" can bring them closer to a "yes" and that every experience, good or bad, contributes to their growth. The ability to persevere in the face of rejection, maintain a positive attitude, and learn from every interaction allows salespeople to move forward and improve every step of the way.

Positive attitude as a catalyst for success

A positive attitude not only helps you cope with challenges, but it also improves the customer experience and fosters a trusting relationship. Salespeople who show enthusiasm and optimism can inspire confidence in their customers and build lasting relationships. Cultivating a positive attitude, even in difficult situations, helps salespeople stay motivated and convey that same spirit to their customers.

Reflection: Success as a journey, not a destination

Success in sales is a **journey of personal** and professional transformation. It's not about reaching a goal and stopping, but about continuing to grow, learn, and adapt throughout your career. Every customer interaction, every challenge overcome, and every technique learned are steps that lead salespeople to become better professionals and more well-rounded people.

This sales journey is an opportunity to develop skills and attitudes that are not only valuable in the workplace, but also in personal life. The ability to listen, adapt, persevere, and constantly improve are skills that enrich salespeople and allow them to face any challenge that life throws at them.

In conclusion, the world of sales is dynamic, and success depends on the willingness of each salesperson to **evolve along with it**. Those who embrace change, invest in its growth, and commit to excellence are destined to achieve success. There are no limits to what a salesperson can accomplish if they are willing to learn, adapt, and do their best every step of the way.

Glossary

This glossary includes key terms commonly used in the sales arena, each of which is essential to understanding and improving the sales process in an organization:

KPI (Key Performance Indicator)
KPIs are **Key Performance Indicators** used to measure and evaluate the success of an activity or process in relation to a specific objective. In sales, KPIs allow you to monitor the performance of the team, such as the number of closed sales, the conversion rate and the average sale value. They are key tools for decision-making and continuous improvement.

Pipeline
The Pipeline, or **Sales Funnel**, is a visual representation of the sales process that shows the different stages that a prospect goes through to become a customer. It includes steps such as prospecting, initial contact, submission of the offer, handling objections, and closing. The Pipeline allows salespeople and managers to visualize the sales pipeline, identify opportunities, and manage activities efficiently.

Role-playing
Role-playing, or role-playing, is a sales training technique where participants take on specific roles (e.g., salesperson and customer) and simulate real sales situations. This exercise allows you to practice skills, such as handling objections, closing sales, and using communication techniques, in a safe environment. It is an effective tool for improving salespeople's skills and preparing them for customer interactions.

PDCA (Plan-Do-Check-Act)
The **PDCA** is a continuous improvement cycle also known as the Deming cycle. It includes four stages:
- **Plan (Plan):** Identify a goal and establish a plan to achieve it.
- **Do:** Implement the plan and execute the actions.
- **Check:** Evaluate the results and compare them with the initial objectives.

- **Act**: Adjust and improve the process based on the results obtained. This cycle is used to optimize sales processes and improve quality in a systematic way.

Lead

A **Lead** is a prospect or potential customer who has shown interest in a product or service. Leads are generated through various marketing and sales strategies, and are the first stage in the pipeline. Leads are qualified and prioritized to determine their conversion potential to customers.

CRM (Customer Relationship Management)

CRM is a **Customer Relationship Management** system that allows businesses to manage interactions with their customers and prospects. A CRM organizes and analyzes customer information, making it easier to track sales opportunities and improve customer satisfaction through personalized attention.

Benchmarking

Benchmarking is the process of comparing a company's sales practices, processes, and metrics with those of industry leaders or direct competitors. This analysis allows you to identify areas for improvement and establish performance standards with the aim of optimizing the sales team's performance.

Prospecting

Prospecting is the process of identifying and qualifying potential customers or leads who may be interested in a company's products or services. It is a critical stage of the pipeline that allows sellers to expand their customer base and increase sales opportunities.

Upselling

Upselling is a sales technique in which the salesperson persuades the customer to buy a more expensive or advanced version of the original product or service. Their goal is to increase the value of the transaction by offering additional features or better benefits.

Cross-selling

Cross-selling, or cross-selling, is a sales technique in which the customer is suggested products or services complementary to the one they are already considering or have purchased. It is an effective strategy to increase the value of each transaction and improve customer satisfaction by offering complete solutions.

Buyer Persona

A **Buyer Persona** is a semi-fictional representation of the ideal customer, based on demographics, behaviors, motivations, and goals of current customers. This tool helps salespeople better understand their customers and adapt their sales strategies to connect more effectively with them.

Objection

An **Objection** is a concern, doubt, or barrier that the customer expresses during the sales process. Objections can be about price, quality, necessity, or time of purchase. Handling objections effectively is crucial to moving the sales process forward and closing the transaction.

Conversion rate

The **Conversion rate** is the percentage of prospects that convert into customers. It is an essential KPI in sales, as it measures the effectiveness of the sales team in transforming opportunities into concrete sales. A high conversion rate indicates that the sales team is managing to capture the interest and trust of prospects.

Lead scoring

Lead scoring is a method of qualifying leads based on specific criteria, such as demographics, online behavior, and interaction history. Leads are scored to identify which ones are most likely to become customers, allowing salespeople to prioritize their efforts and optimize the pipeline.

Sales cycle

The **Sales cycle** is the period of time it takes to complete a sale, from initial contact with the customer to closing. Understanding the sales cycle allows salespeople to manage their time effectively, optimize their strategies, and adjust the pipeline to shorten conversion time.

Sales funnel

The **Sales funnel** is another way of describing the Pipeline, in which prospects go through different stages, from recognizing the problem to making a purchase decision. As they progress, some prospects drop out, so the funnel narrows at each stage, mirroring the process of filtering opportunities.